# TRANSFORMATIONS:

## Readings in Evolution, Hominids, and the Environment

### Edited by Dianne Smith, Ph.D.
### Nicole Slovak, Ph.D.
#### *Santa Rosa Junior College*

**Seventh Edition**

*We travel together, passengers on a little space-ship, dependent on its vulnerable resources of air, water, and soil...preserved from annihilation only by the care, the work and the love we give our fragile craft.*

—Adlai E. Stevenson (1900–1965)

HAYDEN
MCNEIL

Front Cover

*A female baboon grooms a male baboon on the Serengheti plain in Tanzania. Photo by Dianne Smith*

Back Cover (Clockwise from upper left)

*Sweetie, a rescued spider monkey at the Sanctuario Silvestre de Osa in Costa Rica, is seen using her prehensile tail for arboreal stability or balance. Photo by Kinto Diriwacher*

*Sweetie uses grasping digits (toes) to grip a rope at the Sanctuario Silvestre de Osa in Costa Rica. Photo by Heidi Stewart*

*The prehensile tail includes a tactile or sensate pad that has a pattern of ridges and valleys. The tail pad is as individually unique as the human fingerprint. The tactile pad contains nerve tissue and sweat glands that function much as human palms and soles on our hands and feet. Photo by Benjamin Benson*

Printed in the United States of America

10 9 8 7 6 5 4 3 2 1

ISBN 978-0-7380-4374-6

Hayden-McNeil Publishing
14903 Pilot Drive
Plymouth, Michigan 48170
www.hmpublishing.com

SmithD-Slovak 4374-6 F11 (Transformations)

# TRANSFORMATIONS:
*Readings in Evolution, Hominids, and the Environment*

## Introduction

Anthropology and an environmental perspective are inseparable. Human life, indeed our very appearance, was transformed by the specific environments in which we evolved. Today, our cultural habits are transforming all our local and global environments. This complex relationship cannot be fully explained in a simple reader like this, but the issues and data presented here will broaden the reader's exploration of the inseparable transformations that describe the evolution of humanity.

Most individuals think of their family tree as kin they see at holidays and family reunions, or the ancestors they can describe by name, anecdotes, or categories. But each person has a family tree that is much larger than an individual kinship list, and it needs only one name: *hominid*. *Hominid* describes *all human beings and some of our pre-human ancestors*, as well. It is our *scientific* family name.

The origin of hominids remains unclear. Most scientists agree that our family split off from the evolutionary line that led to chimpanzees sometime around 6–7 million years ago, but we are still searching for that last common ancestor. In recent years, hominid discoveries such as *Orrorin tugenensis*, *Sahelanthropus tchadensis*, and *Ardipithecus ramidus* have begun to shed light on hominid origins, but we are still a long way from developing a complete picture of what early hominid life was like.

You and I today are known as *Homo sapiens* or hominids that are modern humans. Together, and with many groups in between, we hominids span about seven million years on earth. The environmental anthropologist instantly sees important similarities and differences between the earliest and most recent hominids. Through this book, the reader will begin to recognize these features as well. Here are a few points to get us started.

What do modern humans share in common with early humanlike beings and other hominids? We both walk upright on our hind limbs; we have larger brains relative

# INTRODUCTION

to body size than other animals; our opposable thumbs allow us to manipulate our material world with strength and finesse; and we depend heavily on our sense of sight to make our way in the habitat. Even though many early hominids were quite small beings—some adults were not quite four feet in height and had smaller brains than we do today—we share all these general hominid features, and thus are kin.

Most anthropologists would agree that we had *culture* throughout our hominid family past as well. *Culture* describes the *behavior and traditions that are learned and shared within social groups*. Significant similarities and differences in learned behavior should be explored between our first ancestors and ourselves, just as we explore our similar and varying biological appearance. Why? Because both culture and biology have been important means of adaptation in our relationship to the environment.

Throughout our past, biological and cultural change—*hominid evolution*—took place as we struggled to extract food from wild sources in our environment and rear our young safely. Our earliest traceable ancestors appear to have occupied forests and woodland areas, as our contemporary primate cousins or apes and most monkeys do today. Nature favored those hominid ancestors that became stable two-legged walkers on the ground, and had larger brains and more agile hands. Their genes were passed on to future generations. We were transformed and became more efficient hunters and gatherers of wild plants and animals. We created tools, weapons, and traditions that would enhance our survival and build our numbers on earth far beyond all other close animal relatives. Our biological changes were linked with greater cultural transformations and by 10,000 years ago, we no longer gathered our food from wild sources; instead, we relied on and continue to rely on an agricultural way of life.

Remarkably, in the larger span of life on earth, our time here is brief. Yet it is a powerful and complicated era that deserves great attention and study at a holistic level. We have become large-brained and intelligent beings, and we no longer extract small elements from our environment to survive biologically. Through our changed biological appearance and our expanded cultural traditions, we use the environment in ways that can and do deplete the very life sources we depend upon for biological survival. Ironically, the very environment that largely transformed

hominid evolution over the last several millions of years is now being transformed by us—a process that has produced both predictable and unforeseen consequences, positive and negative results.

Unraveling human/environmental problems is not an easy task and it cannot be achieved in a single college course. Don't feel frustrated, however, as solutions are underway, and so is your study of them. Through anthropology and environmental studies, one can begin to see the complex web of human life, culture, and nature on earth. Arriving at fresh conclusions and solutions to the environmental dilemmas we face will take time and deliberation. In this text, the reader will accumulate insights from evolutionary theory, genetics, race, disease, nutrition, anatomy, primatology, and paleoanthropology. These are the pieces of the puzzle that anthropologists know make an important picture of human life on earth. They are also keys to use when attempting to resolve environmental problems. It is up to us to study each of these parts and put this picture into clearer focus. When anthropology and the environment are studied together, our understanding of these complex issues can be transformed.

## Note of Gratitude

The editors wish to thank the following anthropologists and faculty for taking the time to provide comments and suggestions on *Transformations*:

Benjamin Benson, M.A.

Margaret Bond, Ph.D.

Jessica Burton, M.A.

Sandra Hollimon, Ph.D.

Michelle Hughes-Markovics, M.A.

Jane Margold, Ph.D.

Laurie Taylor, M.A.

Barbara Wheeler, M.A.

Kent Wisniewski, Ph.D.

# TRANSFORMATIONS:

*Readings in Evolution, Hominids, and the Environment*

# Table of Contents

# TABLE OF CONTENTS

# TABLE OF CONTENTS

# SECTION I:
*Evolution and Human Variation*

# EPISTEMOLOGY:
## *How You Know What You Know*
### Kenneth L. Feder

### Knowing Things

The word *epistemology* means the study of knowledge—how you know what you know. Think about it. How does anybody know anything to be actual, truthful, or real? How do we differentiate fact from fantasy, the reasonable from the unreasonable, the meaningful from the meaningless—in archaeology or in any other field of knowledge? Everybody knows things, but how do we really know these things?

I know, for example, that there is a mountain in a place called Tibet. I know that the mountain is called by Westerners Everest and by Tibetans *Chomolungma* (Goddess of the Universe). I know that it is the tallest land mountain in the world (there are some a bit taller under the ocean). I'm even pretty sure how tall it is: 29,028 feet. But I have never measured it; I've never even been to Tibet. Beyond this, I have not measured all of the other mountains in the world to compare them to Everest. Yet I am quite confident that Everest is the world's tallest peak. But how do I know that?

On the subject of mountains, there is a run-down stone monument on the top of Bear Mountain in the northwestern corner of Connecticut. The monument was built toward the end of the nineteenth century and marks the "highest ground" in Connecticut (*Figure 1.1*). When the monument was built to memorialize this most lofty and auspicious of peaks—the mountain is all of 2,316 feet high—people knew that it was the highest point in the state and wanted to recognize this fact with the monument.

There is only one problem. In recent times, with more accurate, sophisticated measuring equipment, it has been determined that Bear Mountain is not the highest point in Connecticut. The slope of Frissell Mountain, which actually peaks in Massachusetts, reaches a height of 2,380 feet on the Connecticut side of the border, eclipsing Bear Mountain by about 64 feet.

So, people in the late 1800s and early 1900s "knew" that Bear Mountain was the highest point in Connecticut. Today we know that they really did not "know" that, because it was not true—even though they thought it was and built a monument saying so.

Now, suppose that I read in a newspaper, hear on the radio, or see on television a claim that another mountain has been found that is actually 10 (or 50, or 10,000) feet higher than Mount Everest. Indeed, just a few years ago, new satellite data convinced a few, just for a while, that a peak neighboring Everest was, in actuality, slightly higher. That measurement turned out to be in error. But what about the precise height of Everest itself?

**Figure 1.1** *Plaque adorning a stone monument perched atop Bear Mountain in the northwestern corner of Connecticut. Note that the height of the mountain is given as 2,354 feet (it actually is only 2,316 feet) and, in either case, though memorialized as "the highest ground" in the state, it is not. (K. L. Feder)*

Remember my statement that I am "pretty sure" that the height of Everest is 29,028 feet? You will find that number in virtually every book on world geography or geology, in every encyclopedia, and, in fact, in almost every published reference to the great peak—at least before November 1999. That number, 29,028 feet, was, until recently, part of our common knowledge about the world. And it turns out to be wrong, albeit by only a little bit. The quoted figure was determined in 1954 using the best technology available at the time. Our technology for doing such things as measuring elevations has improved radically in the intervening years. In a project sponsored by the National

Geographic Society, a team of climbers ascended Everest in March 1999 to remeasure the "roof of the world." Using information gleaned from Global Positioning System satellites, it was determined that Everest is actually 7 feet higher, 29,035 feet high, and may be growing, if only by a small fraction of an inch each year, as a result of geological forces (Roach 1999).

One of the defining characteristics of science is its pursuit of modification and refinement of what we know and how we explain things. Scientists realize they have to be ever vigilant and, contrary to what some people seem to think, ever open to new information that enables us to tweak, polish, overhaul, or even overturn what we think we know. Science does not grudgingly admit the need for such refinement or reassessment but rather embraces it as a fundamental part of the scientific method.

But now back to Everest. You and I have likely never been to Tibet to personally assess or verify any measurement of the mountain. So what criteria can we use to determine if any of it is true or accurate? It all comes back to epistemology. How, indeed, do we know what we think we know?

## Collecting Information: Seeing Isn't Necessarily Believing

In general, people collect information in two ways:

1. Directly through their own experiences

2. Indirectly through specific information sources such as friends, teachers, parents, books, TV, the Internet, and so forth

People tend to think that obtaining firsthand information—what they see or experience themselves—is always the best way. Unfortunately this is a false assumption because most people are poor observers.

For example, the list of animals that people claim to have observed—and that turn out to be figments of their imagination—is staggering. It is fascinating to read Pliny, a first-century thinker, or Topsell, who wrote in the seventeenth century, and see detailed accounts of the nature and habits of dragons, griffins, unicorns, mermaids, and so on (Byrne 1979). People claimed to have seen these animals, gave detailed descriptions, and even drew pictures of them (*Figure 1.2*). Many folks read their books and believed them.

Nor are untrained observers very good at identifying known, living animals. A red or "lesser" panda escaped from the zoo in Rotterdam, Holland, in December 1978. Red pandas are very rare animals indigenous to China, Tibet, Nepal, and Burma, not Holland. They are distinctive in appearance and cannot be readily mistaken for any other sort of animal. The zoo informed the press that the panda was missing, hoping the publicity would alert people in the area of the zoo and aid in the panda's return. Just when the newspapers came out with the panda story, it was found, quite dead, along some railroad tracks adjacent to the zoo. Nevertheless, over one hundred sightings of the panda *alive* were reported to the zoo from all over the Netherlands *after* the animal was obviously already dead. These reports did not stop until several days after the newspapers announced the discovery of the dead panda (van Kampen 1979). So much for the absolute reliability of firsthand observation.

## Collecting Information: Relying on Others

In exploring the problems of secondhand information, we run into even more complications. When we are not in place to observe something firsthand, we are forced to rely on the quality of someone else's observations, interpretations, and reports—as with the reported height of Mount Everest.

In assessing a report made by others, you need to ask yourself several questions: How did they obtain the information in the first place—revelation, intuition, science?

What are their motives for providing this information? What agenda—religious, philosophical, nationalistic, or otherwise—do they have? What is their source of information, and how expert are they in the topic?

Most people obtain information about the world and current events from established sources such as television news, books, or newspapers. Let's look at the last of these.

Not all newspapers are equally accurate and believable. *The New York Times* has a reputation for factual reporting and carries the following promise in its masthead: "All the News That's Fit to Print." No one, not even their publishers, would characterize tabloid papers like the *Enquirer*, the *Star*, the *Examiner*, the *Weekly World News*, or the *Sun* in those same terms (Bird 1992). When asked about the accuracy of some of the more bizarre stories that appear in his paper, the editor of the *Weekly World News* has been quoted as responding, "For heaven's sake, we entertain people. We make people feel better" (Johnson 1994:27). Notice there is nothing in that response that defends or maintains the accuracy of the stories.

The *Sun* is even more revealing in the disclaimer published in every edition: "*Sun* stories seek to entertain and are about the fantastic, bizarre, and paranormal. The reader should suspend belief for the sake of enjoyment." I presume this means "The reader should suspend *dis*belief for the sake of enjoyment." In other words, leave your skepticism behind because this isn't serious stuff; even we don't

**Figure 1.2** *A seventeenth-century rendition of a clearly mythological beast—a* Mantichora. *The creature was considered to be real and was described as being the size of a wild ass, as having quills on its tail that it could hurl at adversaries, and as having a fondness for human flesh.*

believe most of it. Just read these weird and improbable stories for the entertainment value in them.

In fact, most people follow that advice. In her wonderful anthropological study of the tabloids, S. Elizabeth Bird (1992) shows that most people who read the tabloids regularly do so for the celebrity gossip (which occasionally turns out to be true) and for the uplifting human interest stories that are ignored by the popular press, as well as for the more bizarre material that adorns the pages of these publications. In terms of the latter, regular readers believe some (usually the stuff that reinforces previously held beliefs), but discard most of the rest, viewing it with a combination of interest and humor.

Anthropological topics do attract quite a bit of attention from the tabloids. Mark Allen Peterson (1991), a writer with backgrounds in anthropology and journalism, classifies tabloid stories about anthropology into four categories:

1. *Aliens and ape men*—These stories usually assert some alleged connection between an isolated group of people and extraterrestrial aliens or Bigfoot.

2. *Whacky savages*—These stories focus on the "bizarre" (that term shows up a lot) antics of a tribal or "primitive" people. Sexual and marriage practices are closely scrutinized in these articles.

3. *Whacky anthropologists*—These are usually upbeat stories about anthropologists who are viewed as peculiar and eccentric intellectuals who travel to awful places to study odd, but nevertheless interesting, things.

4. *Silly studies*—These stories are somewhat similar in terms of topic to those included in category 3, but the perspective is quite different, being highly critical of the tax money "wasted" in supporting the frivolous studies conducted by those "whacky anthropologists."

Tabloid stories often are absurd, and few of the writers or even the readers believe them. This still leaves us with the broader question: How do we know what to believe? This is a crucial question that all rational people must ask themselves, whether talking about medicine, religion, archaeology, or anything else. Again, it comes back around to epistemology; how do we know what we think we know, and how do we know what or whom to believe?

## Science: Playing by the Rules

There are ways to knowledge that are both dependable and reliable. We might not be able to get to absolute truths about the meaning of existence, but we can figure out quite a bit about our world— about chemistry and biology, psychology and sociology, physics and history, and even prehistory. The techniques used to get at knowledge we can feel confident in—knowledge that is reliable, truthful, and factual—are referred to as *science*.

In large part, science is a series of techniques used to maximize the probability that what we think we know really reflects the way things are, were, or will be. Science makes no claim to have all the answers or even to be right all the time. On the contrary, during the process of the growth of knowledge and understanding, science is often wrong. Remember that even as seemingly fundamental a fact as the height of the tallest mountain on Earth is subject to reassessment and correction. The only claim that we do make in science is that if we honestly, consistently, and vigorously pursue knowledge using some basic techniques and principles, the truth will eventually surface and we can truly know things about the nature of the world in which we find ourselves.

The question then is, What exactly is science? Hollywood has a number of different stereotypes of scientists. Though there is the occasional female—typically bookish, shy, with thick eyeglasses and hair in a permanent bun—most movie scientist archetypes are white men: the wild-eyed and even wilder-haired eccentric who mixes assorted chemicals in a dark, mysterious laboratory; the brilliant but egotistical young man who misuses the power of his remarkable discovery; the unkempt, nerdy, antisocial genius who is oblivious to the impact his work has on the world. The classic Doctor Frankenstein (*Figure 1.3*) comes immediately to mind.

So much for Hollywood. Scientists are not misfits or megalomaniacs without practical concerns or interests beyond their specialties. We are just people trying to arrive at some truths about how the world and the universe work. Although the application of science can be a slow, frustrating, all-consuming enterprise, the basic assumptions we scientists hold are very simple. Whether we are physicists, biologists, or archaeologists, we all work from four underlying principles. These principles are quite straightforward, but equally quite crucial.

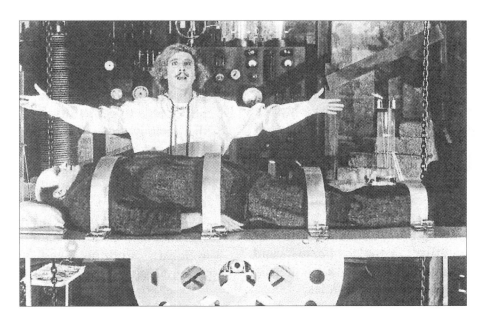

**Figure 1.3** *Gene Wilder depicted a stereotypical—and quite hilarious—mad scientist in the movie* Young Frankenstein. *As funny as his character was, it reflects a common, though quite mistaken, view of what real scientists are like and how they go about their research. (© Motion Picture & TV Photo Archive)*

1. There is a real and knowable universe.

2. The universe (which includes stars, planets, animals, and rocks, as well as people, their cultures, and their histories) operates according to certain understandable rules or laws.

3. These laws are immutable—that means they do not, in general, change depending on where you are or "when" you are.

4. These laws can be discerned, studied, and understood by people through careful observation, experimentation, and research.

Let's look at these assumptions one at a time.

## There Is a Real and Knowable Universe

In science we have to agree that there is a real universe out there for us to study—a universe full of stars, animals, human history, and prehistory that exists whether we are happy with that reality or not.

Recently, it has become fashionable to deny this fundamental underpinning of science. A group of thinkers called *deconstructionists*, for example, believe that all science and

history are merely artificial constructs, devoid of any objective reality or truth. For some deconstructionists, "history exists only in the minds of historians" (Shermer and Grobman 2000:26); the actual past, if there is one, can never be known. As scientists Kurt Gottfried and Kenneth Wilson (1997:545) state, the deconstructionists claim that "scientific knowledge is only a communal belief system with a dubious grip on reality." Deconstructionists try to take apart common beliefs in an attempt to show that much of what we think we know is purely subjective and culturally based.

To some deconstructionists, there is no absolute reality for science to observe or explain; there are only cultural constructs of the universe that are different among people in different societies and even different between men and women within the same culture. There is not one reality but many, and all are equally valid.

Deconstructionists describe science as a purely Western mode of thought, a mechanistic, antinature pattern based on inequality, capitalist exploitation, and patriarchy. The objective observation and understanding at the heart of the scientific approach are impossibilities; the things we see and the explanations we come up with are informed by who we are. (See Paul R. Gross and Norman Levitt's [1994] disturbing book *Higher Superstition: The Academic Left and Its Quarrel with Science* for a detailed criticism of the deconstructionists.) Science, to the deconstructionists, is merely the Western "myth"; it is no more objective and no more "real" than nonscientific myths.

As Theodore Schick and Lewis Vaughn (1999) point out, however, if there is no such thing as objective truth, then no statements, including this one—or any of those made by the deconstructionists themselves—are objectively true. We could know nothing because there would be nothing to know. This is not a useful approach for human beings. Science simply is not the same as myth or oral tradition. Science demands rigorous testing and retesting, and it commonly rejects and discards previous conclusions about the world as a result of such testing. The same cannot be said for nonscientific explanations about how things work.

I suppose one could attempt to demonstrate the culturally subjective nature of the physical principle that two things cannot occupy the same place at the same time by, say, standing in front of a moving train. You probably will not see any deconstructionist attempting this anytime soon.

### The Universe Operates According to Understandable Laws

In essence, what this means is that there are rules by which the universe works: Stars produce heat and light according to the laws of nuclear physics; nothing can go faster than the speed of light; all matter in the universe is attracted to all other matter (the law of gravity).

Though human societies are extremely complex systems and people may not operate according to rigid or unchanging rules of behavior, social scientists can nevertheless construct lawlike generalizations that accurately predict how human groups react to changes in their environment and how their cultures evolve through time. For example, development of complex civilizations in Egypt, China, India/Pakistan, Mesopotamia, Mexico, and Peru was not based on random processes (Haas 1982; Lamberg-Karlovsky and Sabloff 1995). Their evolution seems to reflect similar general patterns. This is not to say that all of these civilizations were identical, any more than we would say that all stars are identical. On the contrary, they existed in different physical and cultural environments, and so we should expect that they would be different.

However, in each case the rise to civilization was preceded by development of an agricultural economy and socially stratified societies. In each case, civilization was also preceded by some degree of overall population increase as well as increased population density in some areas (in other words, the development of cities). Again, in each case we find monumental works (pyramids, temples), evidence of long-distance trade, and development of mathematics, astronomy, and methods of record keeping (usually, but not always, in the form of writing). The cultures in which civilization developed, though some were unrelated and independent, shared these factors because of the nonrandom patterns of cultural evolution.

The point is that everything operates according to rules. In science we believe that by understanding these rules or laws we can understand stars, organisms, and even ourselves.

### The Laws Are Immutable

That the laws do not change under ordinary conditions is a crucial concept in science. A law that works here works there. A law that worked in the past will work today and will work in the future.

For example, if I go to the top of the Leaning Tower of Pisa today and simultaneously drop two balls of unequal mass, they will fall at the same rate and reach the ground at the same time, just as they did when Galileo performed a similar experiment in the seventeenth century. If I perform the same experiment countless times, the same thing will occur because the laws of the universe (in this case, the law of gravity) do not change through time. They also do not change depending on where you are. Go anywhere on the Earth and perform the same experiment—you will get the same results (try not to hit any pedestrians or you will see some other "laws" in operation). This experiment was even performed by U.S. astronauts on the moon during the Apollo 15 mission. A hammer and a feather were dropped from the same height, and they hit the surface at precisely the same instant (the only reason this will not work on Earth is because the feather is caught by the air and the hammer, obviously, is not). We have no reason to believe that the results would be different anywhere or "anywhen" else.

If this assumption of science, that the laws do not change through time, were false, many of the so-called historical sciences, including prehistoric archaeology, could not exist.

For example, historical geologists are interested in knowing how the various landforms we see today came into being. They recognize that they cannot go back in time to see how the Grand Canyon was formed. However, because the laws of geology that governed the development of the Grand Canyon have not changed through time and because these laws are still in operation, historical geologists can study the formation of geological features today and apply what they learn to the past. The same laws they can directly study operating in the present were operating in the past when geological features that interest them first formed.

In the words of nineteenth-century geologist Charles Lyell, the "present" we can observe is the "key" to understanding the past that we cannot. This is true because the laws, or rules, that govern the universe are constant—those that operate today operated in the past. This is why science does not limit itself to the present but makes inferences about the past and even predictions about the future (listen to the weather report for an example of this). We can do so because we can study modern, ongoing phenomena that work under the same laws that existed in the past and will exist in the future.

This is where science and theology are often forced to part company and respectfully disagree. Remember, science depends on the constancy of the laws that we can discern. In contrast, advocates of many religions, though they might believe that there are laws that govern things (and which, according to them, were established by a Creator), usually (but not always) believe that these laws can be changed at any time by their God. In other words, if God does not want the apple to fall to the ground but instead wants it to hover, violating the law of gravity, that is precisely what will happen. As a more concrete example, scientists know that the heat and light given off by a fire result from the transformation of mass (of the wood) to energy. Physical laws control this process. A theologian, however, might agree with this ordinarily but feel that if God wants to create a fire that does not consume any mass (like the "burning bush" seen by Moses in the Old Testament), then this is exactly what will occur. Most scientists simply do not accept this assertion. The rules are the rules. They do not change, even though we might sometimes wish that they would.

## The Laws Can Be Understood

This may be the single most important principle in science. The universe is, theoretically at least, knowable. It may be complicated, and it may take years and years to understand even apparently simple phenomena. Each attempt at understanding leads us to collect more data and to test, reevaluate, and refine our proposed explanations—for how planets formed, why a group of animals became extinct while another thrived, or how a group of ancient people responded to a change in their natural environment, contact with an alien group of people, or adoption of a new technology. We rarely get it right the first time and are continually collecting new information, abandoning some interpretations while refining others. We constantly rethink our explanations. In this way, little by little, bit by bit, we expand our knowledge and understanding. Through this kind of careful observation and objective research and experimentation, we can indeed know things.

So, our assumptions are simple enough. We accept the existence of a reality independent of our own minds, and we accept that this reality works according to a series of unchanging laws or rules. We also claim that we can recognize and understand these laws, or at least recognize the patterns that result from these universal rules. The question remains then: How do we do science—how do we explore the nature of the universe, whether our interest is planets, stars, atoms, or human prehistory?

## The Workings of Science

We can know things by employing the rules of logic and rational thought. Scientists—archaeologists or otherwise—usually work through a combination of the logical processes known as *induction* and *deduction*. The dictionary definition of induction is "arguing from specifics to generalities," whereas deduction is defined as the reverse, arguing from generalities to specifics.

What is essential to good science is objective, unbiased observations—of planets, molecules, rock formations, archaeological sites, and so on. Often, on the basis of these specific observations, we induce explanations called *hypotheses* for how these things work.

For example, we may study the planets Mercury, Venus, Earth, and Mars (each one presents specific bits of information). We then induce general rules about how we think these inner planets in our solar system were formed. Or we might study a whole series of different kinds of molecules and then induce general rules about how all molecules interact chemically. We may study different rock formations and make general conclusions about their origin. We can study a number of specific prehistoric sites and make generalizations about how cultures evolved.

Notice that we cannot directly observe planets forming, the rules of molecular interaction, rocks being made, or prehistoric cultures evolving. Instead, we are inducing general conclusions and principles concerning our data that seem to follow logically from what we have been able to observe.

This process of induction, though crucial to science, is not enough. We need to go beyond our induced hypotheses by testing them. If our induced hypotheses are indeed valid—that is, if they really represent the actual rules according to which some aspect of the universe (planets, molecules, rocks, ancient societies) works—they should be able to hold up under the rigors of scientific hypothesis testing.

Observation and the suggestion of hypotheses, therefore, are only the first steps in a scientific investigation. In science we always need to go beyond observation and hypothesizing. We need to set up a series of "if…then" statements; "if" our hypothesis is true, "then" the following deduced "facts" will also be true. Our results are not always precise and clear-cut, especially in a science like archaeology, but this much should be clear—scientists are not just out there collecting a bunch of interesting facts. Facts are always collected within the context of trying to explain something or of trying to test a hypothesis.

As an example of this logical process, consider the health effects of smoking. How can scientists be sure that smoking is bad for you? After all, it's pretty rare that someone takes a puff on a cigarette and immediately drops dead. The certainty comes from a combination of induction and deduction. Observers have noticed for about 300 years that people who smoked seemed to be more likely to get certain diseases than people who did not smoke. As long ago as the seventeenth century, people noticed that habitual pipe smokers were subject to tumor growths on their lips and in their mouths. From such observations we can reasonably, though tentatively, induce a hypothesis of the unhealthfulness of smoking, but we still need to test

such a hypothesis. We need to set up "if…then" statements. If, in fact, smoking is a hazard to your health (the hypothesis we have induced based on our observations), then we should be able to deduce some predictions that must also be true. Sure enough, when we test specific, deduced predictions such as

1. Smokers will have a higher incidence of lung cancer than nonsmokers

2. Smokers will have a higher incidence of emphysema

3. Smokers will take more sick days from work

4. Smokers will get more upper-respiratory infections

5. Smokers will have diminished lung capacity

6. Smokers will have a shorter life expectancy

We see that our original, induced hypothesis—cigarette smoking is hazardous to your health—is upheld.

That was easy, but also obvious. How about an example with more mystery to it, one in which scientists—acting like detectives—had to solve a puzzle to save lives?

## The Case of Childbed Fever

In nineteenth-century Europe, the hospital could be a very dangerous place for a woman about to give birth. Death rates in some so-called lying-in wards were horrifically high, the result of what became known as "childbed fever." A seemingly healthy young woman would arrive at the hospital with an unremarkable pregnancy, experience a normal labor, and give birth to a healthy baby. Over the course of the hours and days following birth, however, she might exhibit a rapid pulse, high fever, distended and painful abdomen, foul discharge, and delirium—and then would die.

Oddly, while childbed fever took a horrible toll in hospital deliveries, it was rare or absent in home births. In fact, as Sherwin Nuland (2003:97), physician and author of a fascinating book on childbed fever points out, a woman was generally much safer if she gave birth on the street or in an alley on her way to the hospital than if she actually arrived there. For example, carefully maintained mortality statistics show that between 1831 and 1843 in London, approximately 10 out of 10,000 home births resulted in the death of the mother, while in the hospital the death rate was 60 times higher; 600 out of 10,000 died (Nuland 2003:41). In France, similar statistics show that, between 1833 and 1842, the death rate for mothers giving birth in hospitals in Paris was as high as 880 per 10,000 (Nuland 2003:41). By way of comparison, in the United States today, on average, for every 10,000 births there is only about a single maternal death (Chang et al. 2003).

In the nineteenth century, there were two wards, or divisions, at the Vienna General Hospital in Austria. Each year between 6,000 and 7,000 women arrived at the gates of the hospital to give birth, and an equal number ended up in each of the two divisions. In Division 2, in a given year, on average, about 60 women died soon after giving birth, a death rate of about 2 percent. Astonishingly, in Division 1, in the same hospital, the number of yearly deaths was more than ten times higher, with more than 600 and as many as 800 dying in a given year, a terrifying death rate as high as 27 percent (Nuland 2003:97).

Physicians were, needless to say, appalled by such statistics. Performing autopsies on patients who had died in the hospital had become a regular practice in the nineteenth century in Europe. Many doctors carefully examined the bodies of the women who had died of childbed fever and found them ravaged by an aggressive infection and filled with an intensely foul smelling whitish fluid. Many of these physicians were more than willing to propose hypotheses suggesting possible causes of the condition. Perhaps, it was suggested, tight petticoats worn early in pregnancy were involved, leading to a woman's inability to expel fluids after giving birth. Or perhaps it was the foul air in hospitals with their closed-in spaces. Magnetic fields and atmospheric disturbances were blamed. Perhaps some women simply were predisposed to having their milk ducts get blocked and then dying when milk deteriorated inside of them; the whiteness of the infection seen in autopsy was assumed by some to indicate its source as soured mother's milk. Others, aware that home births with their very low rates of childbed fever were attended to by midwives, all of whom were themselves women, suggested that the condition was the result of female modesty.

In other words, childbed fever afflicted women who were particularly embarrassed by being examined by male doctors and medical students. Some even proposed the wonderfully circular explanation that childbed fever had a psychological origin, the result of the great fear many women had of the hospital because of the possibility of contracting childbed fever!

Back in Vienna at the General Hospital, Ignaz Semmelweis, a young Hungarian doctor who had been turned down for a couple of plum assignments, ended up, by default, in obstetrics. Determined to solve the childbed fever riddle, Semmelweis realized that the General Hospital, with its two divisions having very different mortality rates, presented a unique opportunity to experimentally test the various hypotheses proposed to explain childbed fever.

Semmelweis immediately rejected those proposed explanations that didn't differentiate the two divisions. For example, one doctor suggested that childbed fever was caused by badly maintained hospital walls, but the walls were in equal disrepair in both divisions, and the mortality rates were entirely different, so it was pointless to pursue this explanation. While outright rejecting hypotheses related to atmospheric conditions, earth energies, and dirty walls, Semmelweis and some of his colleagues at the hospital recognized a handful of genuine and potentially important differences between the two obstetrical divisions in the hospital and induced a series of possible explanations for the drastic difference in their mortality rates. They suggested:

1. Division 1 tended to be more crowded than Division 2. The overcrowding in Division 1 was a possible cause of the higher mortality rate there.

2. Women in Division 2 were assisted by midwives who directed the women to deliver on their sides, while those in Division 1 were attended to by physicians and medical students who kept women on their backs during delivery. Birth position was a possible cause of the higher mortality rate.

3. There was a psychological factor involved; the hospital priest had to walk through Division 1 to administer the last rites to dying patients in other wards. Perhaps this sight so upset some women already weakened by the ordeal of childbirth that it contributed to their deaths.

4. Unlike the women in Division 2, who were assisted by experienced midwives using far less invasive techniques, the women in Division 1 were attended to by medical students being trained in obstetrics. Perhaps all of the additional poking and prodding conducted during this training was harmful and contributed to the higher death rate of women in Division 1.

These induced hypotheses all sounded good. Each marked a genuine difference between Divisions 1 and 2 that might have caused the difference in the death rate. Semmelweis was doing what most scientists do in such a situation; he was relying on creativity and imagination in seeking out an explanation.

Creativity and imagination are just as important to science as good observation. But being creative and imaginative was not enough. It did not help the women who were still dying at an alarming rate. Semmelweis had to go beyond producing possible explanations; he had to test each one of them. So, he deduced the necessary implications of each:

1.  If hypothesis 1 were correct, then alleviating the crowding in Division 1 should reduce the mortality rate. The result: no change. So the first hypothesis was rejected. It had failed the scientific test; it simply could not be correct.

2.  Semmelweis went on to test hypothesis 2 by changing the birth positions of the women in Division 1 to match those of the women in Division 2. Again, there was no change, and another hypothesis was rejected.

3   Next, to test hypothesis 3, the priest was rerouted. Women in Division 1 continued to die of childbed fever at about five times the rate of those in Division 2.

4.  To test hypothesis 4, it was decided to limit the number of invasive procedures used on the women to train the students in their examination techniques. This was accomplished by limiting the number of students who actually examined the women. Specifically, the many non-Austrian students in the obstetrics program were restricted from examining these patients, while the native Austrians continued to be trained in the ward. The statistics showed that this had no impact on the death rate in Division 1; 10 or 11 percent of the women continued to die even when fewer students were allowed to examine them internally.

Then, as so often happens in science, Semmelweis had a stroke of luck. An acquaintance—also a doctor—died, and the manner of his death provided Semmelweis with another possible explanation for the problem in Division 1. Though Semmelweis's friend was not a woman who had recently given birth, he did have precisely the same symptoms as did the women who were dying of childbed fever. Most important, this doctor had died of a disease similar to childbed fever soon after accidentally cutting himself during an autopsy.

Viruses and bacteria were unknown in the 1840s. Surgical instruments were not sterilized, no special effort was made to clean the hands, and doctors did not wear gloves during operations and autopsies. Supposing that there was something bad in dead bodies and this something had entered Semmelweis's friend's system through his wound— could the same bad "stuff" (Semmelweis called it "cadaveric material") get onto the hands of the physicians and medical students, who then might, without washing, go on to help a woman give birth? Then, if this "cadaveric material" were transmitted into the woman's body during the birth of her baby, it might lead to her death.

This possibility inspired Semmelweis's final hypothesis: The presence of physicians and medical students in Division 1 was at the root of the mystery. Students who attended the women in Division 1 regularly conducted autopsies as part of their training and so would be in contact with dead bodies on the same days they were assisting women giving birth. Furthermore, physicians would frequently perform autopsies on the bodies of women who had already died of childbed fever, often going directly from the autopsy room to the birthing rooms to assist other women giving birth. Herein was a grimly ironic twist to this new hypothesis; the attempt by physicians to solve the mystery of childbed fever by performing autopsies on its victims was one of the most important factors in transmitting the disease to additional women.

To test this hypothesis, Semmelweis instituted new policies in Division 1, including the requirement that all attending physicians and students cleanse their hands with chlorine before entering. The result: The death rate among women birthing in Division 1 dropped to between 1 and 2 percent, exactly the rate in Division 2. Semmelweis had both solved the mystery and halted an epidemic.

## Science and Nonscience: The Essential Differences

Through objective observation and analysis, a scientist, whether a physicist, chemist, biologist, psychologist, or archaeologist, sees things that need explaining. Through creativity and imagination, the scientist suggests possible hypotheses to explain these "mysteries." The scientist then sets up a rigorous method through experimentation or subsequent research to deductively test the validity of a given hypothesis. If the implications of a hypothesis are shown not to be true, the hypothesis must be rejected and then it's back to the drawing board. If the implications are found to be true, we can uphold or support our hypothesis.

A number of other points should be made here. The first is that for a hypothesis, whether it turns out to be upheld or not, to be scientific, it must be testable. In other words, there must be clear, deduced implications that can be drawn from the hypothesis and then tested. Remember the hypotheses of "magnetic fields" and "atmospheric disturbances"? How can you test these? What are the necessary implications that can be deduced from the hypothesis "More women died in Division 1 because of atmospheric disturbances"? There really aren't any, and therefore such a hypothesis is not scientific—it cannot be tested. Remember, in the methodology of science, we ordinarily need to

1.  Observe

2.  Induce general hypotheses or possible explanations for what we have observed

3.  Deduce specific things that must also be true if our hypothesis is true

4.  Test the hypothesis by checking out the deduced implications

As Michael Shermer (1997:19) points out, "Science, of course, is not this rigid, and no scientist consciously goes through 'steps.' The process is a constant interaction of making observations, drawing conclusions, making predictions, and checking them against evidence."

Testing a hypothesis is crucial. If there are no specific implications of a hypothesis that can then be analyzed as a test of the validity or usefulness of that hypothesis, then you simply are not doing and cannot do "science."

For example, suppose you observe a person who appears to be able to "guess" the value of a playing card picked from a deck. Next, assume that someone hypothesizes that "psychic" ability is involved. Finally, suppose the claim is made that the "psychic" ability goes away as soon as you try to test it (actually named the "shyness effect" by some researchers of the paranormal). Such a claim is not itself testable and therefore not scientific.

Beyond the issue of testability, another lesson is involved in determining whether an approach to a problem is scientific. Semmelweis induced four different hypotheses to explain the difference in mortality rates between Divisions 1 and 2. These "competing" explanations are called *multiple working hypotheses*. Notice that Semmelweis did not simply proceed by a process of elimination. He did not, for example, test the first three hypotheses and—after finding them invalid—declare that the fourth was necessarily correct because it was the only one left that he had thought of.

Some people try to work that way. A light is seen in the sky. Someone hypothesizes it was a meteor. We find out that it was not. Someone else hypothesizes that it was a military rocket. Again this turns out to be incorrect. Someone else suggests that it was the Goodyear blimp, but that turns out to have been somewhere else. Finally, someone suggests that it was the spacecraft of people from another planet. Some will say that this must be correct because none of the other explanations panned out. This is nonsense. There are plenty of other possible explanations. Eliminating all of the explanations we have been able to think of except one (which, perhaps, has no testable implications) in no way allows us to uphold that final hypothesis. You will see just such an error in logic with regard to the Shroud of Turin artifact discussed in Chapter 16.

## A Rule in Assessing Explanations

Finally, there is hypothesis making another rule and testing. It is called *Occam's razor* or *Occam's rule*. In thinking, in trying to solve a problem, or in attempting to explain some phenomenon, "Entities are not to be multiplied beyond necessity." In other words, the explanation or hypothesis that explains a series of observations with the fewest other assumptions or leaps—the hypothesis that does not multiply these entities beyond necessity—is the best explanation.

Here's an example. My archaeology class was to begin in about ten minutes, and the previous class was just dispersing from what had obviously been a raucous session. As I entered the room, I noticed the three-dimensional, geometric shapes made of heavy stock paper suspended by string from the seminar room ceiling. I caught the attention of the professor, a truly gentle soul and one of the nicest people I had met in my first year of teaching, and I asked the obvious question: "What's the deal with the shapes?" She smiled and launched into a passionate discourse about the exercise just conducted by the class—an experiment in "psychokinesis," the ostensible ability to move or otherwise affect objects simply by the power of thought. Perhaps my jaw dropped a little too obviously, and my colleague asked, "Would you like to see me do it?" Without waiting for a response, she gazed up at the shape directly above her head and closed her eyes; when she opened them we both looked up to see the suspended object swaying back and forth. "See?" she said.

Before you get too terribly excited about this demonstration, perhaps I should add that it was a rather breezy day and the windows in the seminar room were wide open. The object toward which my colleague had directed her ostensibly paranormal talents indeed was moving, but so were all of the other suspended objects, as were papers on the desk at the front of the class and just about anything else that wasn't nailed down. I pointed out that, just perhaps, the suspended object was moving simply because of the wind. My colleague just smiled broadly, patted me on the shoulder, and said, "Oh Kenny, you're such a skeptic." Indeed I am, and in this story rests the essence of Occam's razor. Could the object have been moving as the result of my colleague's psychokinetic prowess? Well, yes. But it also could have been moving as a result of open windows and wind. Which explanation— psychokinesis or wind—requires the least violence to our understanding of reality? Which requires the fewest logical leaps or as yet unsupported assumptions about how the universe operates? Occam's razor directs the gambler in reality's casino to bet on the sure thing or, at least, the surer thing, until a preponderance of evidence convinces one otherwise. In this particular case, I'm betting on the wind.

Here's another example. During the eighteenth and nineteenth centuries, huge buried, fossilized bones were found throughout North America and Europe (*Figure 1.4*). One hypothesis, the simplest, was that the bones were the remains of animals that no longer existed. This hypothesis simply relied on the assumption that bones do not come into existence by themselves but always serve as the skeletons of animals. Therefore, when you find bones, there must have been animals who used those bones. However, another hypothesis was suggested: The bones were deposited by the Devil to fool us into thinking that such animals existed (Howard 1975). This hypothesis "multiplied" those "entities" Occam warned us about. This explanation demanded many more assumptions about the universe than did the first: There is a Devil, that Devil is interested in human affairs, he wants to fool us, he has the ability to make bones of animals that never existed, and he has the ability to hide them under the ground and inside solid rock. That is quite a number of unproven (and largely untestable) claims to swallow.

**Figure 1.4** *An 1827 lithograph of a fossil quarry in the Tilgate Forest, Sussex, England. Workers are extracting a dinosaur bone from a large rock fragment. (From Mantell's* Geology of Sussex)

Thus, Occam's razor says the simpler hypothesis, that these great bones are evidence of the existence of animals that no longer exist—in other words, dinosaurs—is better. The other explanation raises more questions than it answers.

## The Art of Science

Don't get the impression that science is a mechanical enterprise. Science is at least partially an art. It is much more than just observing the results of experiments.

It takes great creativity to recognize a "mystery" in the first place. In the apocryphal story, countless apples had fallen from countless trees and undoubtedly conked the noggins of multitudes of stunned individuals who never thought much about it. It took a fabulously creative individual, Isaac Newton, to even recognize that herein lay a mystery. Why did the apple fall? It could have hovered in midair. It could have moved off in any of the cardinal directions. It could have gone straight up and out of sight. But it did not. It fell to the ground as it always had, in all places, and as it always would. It took great imagination to recognize that in this simple observation (and in a bump on the head) rested the eloquence of a fundamental law of the universe.

## Where Do Hypotheses Come From?

Coming up with hypotheses is not a simple or mechanical procedure. The scientific process requires creativity. Hypotheses arrive as often in flashes of insight as through plodding, methodical observation. Consider this example.

My field crew and I had just finished excavating the 2,000-year-old Loomis II archaeological site in Connecticut where a broad array of different kinds of stones had been used for making tools. Some of the "lithics" came from sources close to the site. Other sources were located at quite a distance, as much as a few hundred miles away. These nonnative "exotic" lithics were universally superior; tools could be made more easily from the nonlocal materials, and the edges produced were much sharper.

At the time the site was being excavated, I noticed that there seemed to be a pattern in terms of the size of the individual tools we were recovering. Tools made from the locally available and generally inferior materials of quartz and basalt were relatively large, and the pieces of rock that showed no evidence of use—archaeologists call

these discarded pieces *debitage*—were also relatively large. In contrast, the tools made from the superior materials—a black flint and two kinds of jasper—that originated at a great distance from the site were much smaller. Even inconsequential flakes of exotic stone—pieces you could barely hold between two fingers—showed evidence of use, and only the tiniest of flakes was discarded without either further modification for use or evidence of use, such as for scraping, cutting, or piercing.

I thought it was an interesting pattern but didn't think much of it until about a year later when I was cleaning up the floor of my lab after a class in experimental archaeology where students were replicating stone tools. We used a number of different raw materials in the class, and just as was the case for the site, stone of inferior quality was readily available a few miles away, whereas more desirable material was from more distant sources.

As I cleaned up, I noticed that the discarded stone chips left by the students included perfectly serviceable pieces of the locally available, easy-to-obtain stone, and only the tiniest fragments of flint and obsidian. We obtained flint in New York State from a source about 80 miles from campus, and we received obsidian from Wyoming. Suddenly it was clear to me that the pattern apparent at the archaeological site was repeating itself nearly two thousand years later among my students. More "valuable" stone—functionally superior and difficult to obtain—was used more efficiently, and there was far less waste than in stone that was easy to obtain and more difficult to work. I could now phrase this insight as a hypothesis and test it using the site data: More valuable lithic materials were used more efficiently at the Loomis II archaeological site (Feder 1981). In fact, by a number of measurements, this turned out to be precisely the case. The hypothesis itself came to me when I wasn't thinking of anything in particular; I was simply sweeping the floor.

It may take great skill and imagination to invent a hypothesis in the attempt to understand why things seem to work the way they do. Remember, Division 1 at the Vienna General Hospital did not have written over its doors, "Overcrowded Division" or "Division with Student Doctors Who Don't Wash Their Hands After Autopsies." It took imagination, first, to recognize that there were differences between the divisions and, second, to hypothesize that some of the differences might logically be at the root of the mystery. After all, there were in all likelihood many differences between the divisions: their compass orientations, the names of the nurses, the precise alignment of the windows, the astrological signs of the doctors who worked in the divisions, and so on. If a scientist were to attempt to test all of these differences as hypothetical causes of a mystery, nothing would ever be solved. Occam's razor must be applied. We need to focus our intellectual energies on those possible explanations that require few other assumptions. Only after all of these have been eliminated can we legitimately consider others. As summarized by that great fictional detective, Sherlock Holmes:

> It is of the highest importance in the art of detection to be able to recognize, out of a number of facts, which are incidental and which are vital. Otherwise, your energy and attention must be dissipated instead of being concentrated. (Doyle 1891–1902:275)

Semmelweis concentrated his attention on first four, then a fifth possible explanation. Like all good scientists he had to use some amount of what we can call "intuition" to sort out the potentially vital from the probably incidental. Even in the initial sorting we may be wrong. Overcrowding, birth position, and psychological trauma seemed like very plausible explanations to Semmelweis, but they were wrong nonetheless.

## Testing Hypotheses

Finally, it takes skill and inventiveness to suggest ways for testing the hypothesis in question. We must, out of our own heads, be able to invent the "then" part of our "if... then" statements. We need to be able to suggest those things that must be true if our hypothesis is to be supported. There really is an art to that. Anyone can claim there was a Lost Continent of Atlantis (Chapter 7), but often it takes a truly inventive mind to suggest precisely what archaeologists must find if the hypothesis of its existence is indeed to be validated.

Semmelweis tested his hypotheses and solved the mystery of childbed fever by changing conditions in Division 1 to see if the death rate would change. In essence, testing each hypothesis was an experiment.

It might seem obvious that medical researchers, physicists, or chemists working in labs can perform experiments, observe the results, and come to reasonable conclusions about what transpired. But how about the historical disciplines, including historical geology, history, and prehistoric archaeology? Researchers in these fields cannot go back in time to be there when the events they are attempting to describe and explain took place. Can they really know what happened in the past?

Yes, they can, by what historians Michael Shermer and Alex Grobman (2000:32) call a "convergence of evidence." For example, in their book *Denying History: Who Says the Holocaust Never Happened and Why Do They Say It?* they respond to those who deny that the Germans attempted to exterminate the Jewish population of Europe in the 1930s and 1940s. After all, even though that era isn't ancient history, we still can't return to observe it for ourselves, so how do we know what really happened? Shermer and Grobman marshal multiple sources of evidence, including documents like letters, speeches, blueprints, and articles where Germans discussed their plans; eyewitness accounts of individual atrocities; photographs showing the horror of the camps; the physical remains of the camps themselves; inferential evidence like demographic data showing that approximately 6 million European Jews disappeared during this period. Though we cannot travel back in time to the 1940s, these different and independent lines of evidence converge, allowing us to conclude with absolute certainty that a particular historical event—in this case, the Holocaust—actually happened. Indeed, we can know what happened in history—and prehistory.

Ultimately, whether a science is experimentally based or not makes little logical difference in testing hypotheses. Instead of predicting what the results of a given experiment must be if our induced hypothesis is useful or valid, we predict what new data we must be able to find if a given hypothesis is correct.

For instance, we may hypothesize that long-distance trade is a key element in the development of civilization based on our analysis of the ancient Maya. We deduce that if this is correct—if this is, in fact, a general rule of cultural evolution—then we must find large quantities of trade items in other parts of the world where civilization also developed. We might further deduce that these items should be found in contexts that denote their value and importance to the society (for example, in the burials of leaders). We must then determine the validity of our predictions and, indirectly, our hypothesis by going out and conducting more research. We need to excavate sites belonging to other ancient civilizations and see if they

**Table 1.1** Books that explain the Scientific Method

| Author | Book Title | Year | Publisher |
|--------|-----------|------|-----------|
| Stephen Carey | *A Beginner's Guide to Scientific Method* | 1998 | Wadsworth |
| Thomas Gilovich | *How We Know What Isn't So* | 1991 | Free Press |
| Howard Kahane | *Logic and Contemporary Rhetoric: The Use of Reason in Everyday Life* | 1998 | Wadsworth |
| Robert Park | *Voodoo Science: The Road from Foolishness to Fraud Press* | 2000 | Oxford University |
| Daisie Radner and Michael Radner | *Science and Unreason* | 1982 | Wadsworth |
| Milton Rothman | *The Science Gap: Dispelling Myths and Understanding the Reality of Science* | 1992 | Prometheus Books |
| Carl Sagan | *The Demon-Haunted World* | 1996 | Random House |
| Michael Shermer | *Why People Believe Weird Things* | 1997 | W. H. Freeman |
| Theodore Schick and Lewis Vaughn | *Thinking About Weird Things: Critical Thinking for a New Age* | 1999 | Mayfield |
| Lewis Wolpert | *The Unnatural Nature of Science* | 1993 | Harvard University Press |
| Charles Wynn and Arthur Wiggins | *Quantum Leaps in the Wrong Direction* | 2001 | Joseph Henry Press |

followed the same pattern as seen for the Maya relative to the importance of trade.

Testing of hypotheses takes a great deal of thought, and we can make mistakes. We must remember: We have a hypothesis, we have the deduced implications, and we have the test. We can make errors at any place within this process—the hypothesis may be incorrect, the implications may be wrong, or the way we test them may be incorrect. Scientists are not perfect, and biases and preconceptions can interfere with this process. Certainty in science is a scarce commodity. There are always new hypotheses, alternative explanations, and more deductive implications to test. Nothing is ever finished, nothing is set in concrete, nothing is ever defined or raised to the level of religious truth.

## The Human Enterprise of Science

Science is a very human endeavor practiced by imperfect human beings. Scientists are not isolated from the cultures and times in which they live. They share many of the same prejudices and biases of other members of their societies.

Scientists learn from mentors at universities and inherit their perspectives. It often is quite difficult to go against the scientific grain, to question accumulated wisdom, and to suggest a new approach or perspective.

Consider the case of meteors. Today we take it for granted that sometimes quite large, extraterrestrial, natural objects go streaking across the sky and sometimes even strike the ground (then they are called meteorites). You may even be aware that major meteor showers can be seen twice a year: the Perseid shower in August and the Leonid shower in November. Perhaps you have been lucky enough to see a major meteor or "bolide," an awesome example of nature's fireworks. But until about two hundred years ago the notion that solid stone or metallic objects originating in space regularly enter the Earth's atmosphere and sometimes strike the ground was controversial and, in fact, rejected by most scientists. In 1704 Sir Isaac Newton categorically rejected the notion that there could be meteors because he did not believe there could be any cosmological source for them.

The quality of an argument and the evidence marshalled in its support should be all that matters in science. The authority or reputation of the scientist should not matter. Nevertheless, not many scientists were willing to go against the considered opinion of as bright a scientific luminary as Isaac Newton. Even so, a few brave thinkers risked their reputations by concluding that meteors really did originate in outer space. Their work was roundly criticized, at least for a time. But science is "self-corrective." Hypotheses are constantly being refined and retested as new data are collected.

In 1794, over the skies of Siena, Italy, there was a spectacular shower of about three thousand meteors, seen by tens of thousands of people (Cowen 1995). Even then, a nonmeteoric explanation was suggested. By coincidence, Mount Vesuvius had erupted just eighteen hours before the shower, and some tried to blame the volcano for being the source of the objects flaming in the skies over Italy.

Critics did what they could to dispel the "myth" of an extraterrestrial source for the streaks of light over Siena, but they could not succeed. Further investigation of subsequent major meteor falls in the late 1700s and early 1800s, as well as examination of the chemical makeup of some of the objects that had actually fallen from the sky (an iron and nickel alloy not found on Earth), convinced most by the early nineteenth century that meteors are what we now know them to be—extraterrestrial chunks of stone or metal that flame brightly when they enter our planet's atmosphere.

Philosopher of science Thomas Kuhn (1970) has suggested that the growth of scientific knowledge is not neatly linear, with knowledge simply building on knowledge. He maintains that science remains relatively static for periods and that most thinkers work under the same set of assumptions—the same *paradigm*. New ideas or perspectives, like those of Semmelweis or Einstein, that challenge the existing orthodoxy are usually initially rejected. Only once scientists get over the shock of the new ideas and start testing the new frameworks suggested by these new paradigms are great jumps in knowledge made.

That is why in science we propose, test, tentatively accept, but never prove a hypothesis. We keep only those hypotheses that cannot be disproved. As long as a hypothesis holds up under the scrutiny of additional testing through experiment and is not contradicted by new data, we accept it as the best explanation so far. Some hypotheses sound good, pass the rigors of initial testing, but are later shown to be inadequate or invalid. Others—for example, the hypothesis of biological evolution—have held up so well (all new data either were or could have been deduced from it) that they will probably always be upheld. We usually call these very well supported hypotheses *theories*. However, it is in the nature of science that no matter how well an explanation of some aspect of reality has held up, we must always be prepared to consider new tests and better explanations.

We are interested in knowledge and explanations of the universe that work. As long as these explanations work, we keep them. As soon as they cease being effective because new data and tests show them to be incomplete or misguided, we discard them and seek new ones. In one sense, Semmelweis was wrong after all, though his explanation worked at the time—he did save lives through its application. We now know that there is nothing inherently bad in "cadaveric material." Dead bodies are not the cause of childbed fever. Today we realize that it is bacteria that can grow in the flesh of a dead body that can get on a doctor's hands, infect a pregnant woman, and cause her death. Semmelweis worked in a time before the existence of such things was known. Science in this way always grows, expands, and evolves. See *Table 1.1* for a number of works that discuss the method of science.

## Science and Archaeology

The study of the human past is a science and relies on the same general logical processes that all sciences do. Unfortunately, perhaps as a result of its popularity, the data of archaeology have often been used by people to attempt to prove some idea or claim. Too often, these attempts have been bereft of science.

# 2 EVOLUTION AS FACT, THEORY AND PATH

## T. Ryan Gregory

### Introduction

With its vocabulary of hundreds of thousands of words, one might expect English to boast a surplus of ways to express different concepts. Indeed, there are many well-known examples of multiple descriptors for the same item or idea, often one or more from the Germanic and others from the Latinate roots of modern English. In addition to the diversity resulting from a history of linguistic hybridization, English has a tendency to assimilate words from other languages and to include the *de novo* creation of terms as the need arises. Thus, most technically complex professions exhibit a plethora of neologisms and jargon that can be all but impenetrable to nonexperts. Science is certainly no exception in this regard.

However, when it comes to some of the most fundamental concepts in science, there is a dearth of unambiguous terminology. Worse still, words with relatively clear meanings in the vernacular are employed with very different definitions in science, a phenomenon that greatly confuses discussions of science when they are conducted in nonscientific contexts. For example, terms such as "energy" or "force" have specific meanings in physics that are easily confused when commingled with their common usages. This ambiguity has been exploited to considerable advantage by many a huckster who falsely invokes the respectability of science in the sale of products that would, in actuality, contradict well-established scientific principles if they really exerted any of their claimed effects.

Even more generally, terms relating to the process and products of science itself, such as "theory" and "law," are almost diametrically opposite in scientific vs vernacular settings. This has been a source of both honest confusion and intentional obfuscation in discussions of science, especially with regard to evolution—which has, with the full thrust of equivocation, been misleadingly labeled as "just a theory" by opponents for decades. The intent of this article is to clarify the general meaning of some central concepts in science and the terms used to describe them, and to differentiate these from the very different definitions of the same words in common usage. The specific application of these terms, as defined in science, to the topic of evolution will be discussed in some detail.

## Defining Terms

Hypothesis, theory, fact, law. Prefaced with "hunch" or "guess," this list of terms would reflect what many people consider a graded series from least to greatest degree of certainty. This ranking may be appropriate in common usage, but actually makes little sense when these words are employed in a scientific context.

### Fact

"Fact" is perhaps the only term in the above list whose common and technical definitions are similar. The major difference is in the degree of certainty expressed, which is simultaneously higher and lower in scientific usage. Following the definition provided by the US National Academy of Science (NAS) (1998), one of the most prestigious scientific societies in the world, a scientific fact is "an observation that has been repeatedly confirmed, and for all practical purposes, is accepted as 'true.'" Or, as Stephen Jay Gould (1981) put it in his inimitable style, "In science, 'fact' can only mean 'confirmed to such a degree that it would be perverse to withhold provisional assent.'" It is this insistence on repeated confirmation by data—either through direct observation or reliable inference—that makes a claim to "fact" so much stronger in science. However, as the NAS points out, "truth in science is never final, and what is accepted as a fact today may be modified or even discarded tomorrow." Small-scale details are regularly revised as more precise observations are made, whereas well-established facts of fundamental significance are very rarely overthrown, but in principle, no scientific fact of any magnitude is beyond revision or refutation. As a result, scientists must maintain a balance between the confidence that comes from reinforcing conclusions about the world with repeatable data and the understanding that absolute certainty is not something that the methods of science are able or intended to deliver.

### Theory

The common and scientific definitions of "theory," unlike of "fact," are drastically different. In daily conversation, "theory" often implicitly indicates a *lack* of supporting data. Indeed, introducing a statement with "My theory is..." is usually akin to saying "I guess that..." "I would speculate that..." or "I believe but have not attempted to demonstrate that..." By contrast, a theory in science, again following the definition given by the NAS, is "a well-substantiated explanation of some aspect of the natural world that can incorporate facts, laws, inferences, and tested hypotheses." Science not only generates facts but seeks to explain them, and the interlocking and well-supported explanations for those facts are known as theories. Theories allow aspects of the natural world not only to be described, but to be understood. Far from being unsubstantiated speculations, theories are the ultimate goal of science.

### Hypothesis

The validity of scientific theories is not determined solely by their ability to accommodate and account for known facts. Theories also are actively tested, and it is here that "hypotheses" play an important role. According to the NAS, a scientific hypothesis is "a tentative statement about the natural world leading to deductions that can be tested." Testing can involve direct experimentation or the generation of predictions about as-yet-unobserved facts that can be evaluated by further observation. This latter process plays a significant part in the validation of theories in sciences such as astronomy and geology where direct experimental manipulation is difficult. As the NAS notes, "If the deductions are verified, the hypothesis is provisionally corroborated. If the deductions are incorrect, the original hypothesis is proved false and must be abandoned or modified." It bears noting that the rejection of a hypothesis does not automatically imply the refutation of an entire theory because hypotheses are usually sufficiently focused to test only one aspect of complex theories.

### Law

Finally, "law," for which, once again, there is a nearly opposite definition in everyday use compared to the application of the term in science. "Laws," in normal experience, are *prescriptive*—that is, they dictate what behaviors one should carry out and which ones must be avoided. A posted speed limit, for example, (attempts to) dictate the behaviors of drivers. A scientific law, on the other hand, is *descriptive*—it is a "generalization about how some aspect of the natural world behaves under stated circumstances," according to the NAS. In the vernacular, a law *prescribes* behavior and limits what is permitted to happen. In science, a law *describes* and predicts what will happen when the range of possible conditions is limited. If one is caught speeding, then mechanisms are implemented to correct this deviation from externally imposed limits. However, there is no punishment for "violating the laws of physics" or "defying the law of gravity" because these phrases are nonsensical from a scientific standpoint.

More specifically, if an observation does not conform to the expectations of a scientific law, then either (1) the observation was illusory or interpreted incorrectly, (2) the observed event took place outside the specified conditions to which the law applies, or (far less likely), (3) the law is inaccurately formulated. A prime example is provided by the chronically misunderstood Second Law of Thermodynamics, which states that "the entropy of a closed system not in equilibrium will tend to increase over time, approaching a maximum value at equilibrium." In this case, the conditions are very clearly specified: if there is no external source of energy ("a closed system"), then there will be a net increase in disorder until the system reaches equilibrium. Local increases in order are not precluded (ornate snowflakes still form from water vapor), and of course, this does not apply to living things, which draw energy from their environments (and ultimately from the sun), and hence, represent open systems. Readers of this article establish this latter claim conclusively, having passed from a simple zygote to a complex organism composed of trillions of specialized cells. If the Second Law of Thermodynamics implied that all natural increases in order were impossible, then it would be incorrect. It does not and (so far as we know) is not. The broader point is that invoking the Second Law of Thermodynamics as an argument against evolution reveals a misunderstanding of both the scope of this particular law and of the meaning of "law" in science generally.

Theories explain facts and are tested by generating hypotheses. No matter how much information accrues, hypotheses never become theories, and theories never graduate into laws. These terms describe three distinct aspects of science.

## An Attractive Case Study

The scientific application of words that are used in very different ways under normal circumstances can appear rather counterintuitive, to be sure. In this sense, it is instructive to consider a case study with which all readers of this article are at least casually familiar: gravity. Some facts—observations repeatedly confirmed and considered accurate—about gravity include the following:

1. Even though the Earth is rotating rapidly, physical objects on its surface (say, readers of this article) are not flung off into space.

2. If one drops something or throws it into the air, it falls to the ground.

3. Objects dropped in the same location accelerate under gravity at the same rate, regardless of their mass (wind resistance notwithstanding).

The first of these is being observed and confirmed at this very moment all over the planet. The second can be tested at any time (feel free to confirm it using a nonbreakable object of your choosing). The third is far less intuitive, and in fact, required the genius of Galileo to demonstrate as a scientific principle and subsequent researchers with more sophisticated instruments to confirm. The equal rates of acceleration of objects independent of mass can be demonstrated by using objects of similar shape (to cancel out differences in friction with the air—try, say, a baseball and a basketball; Galileo used balls rolling down inclines), and this can be observed using any objects in an artificially created vacuum. However, one of the most dramatic demonstrations came when Dave Scott, an astronaut on the Apollo 15 mission to the airless surface of the moon, dropped a hammer and a feather and observed the result. "How about that," he noted, "Mr. Galileo was correct."

Gravity cannot be observed directly, such that its characteristics must be inferred from observations of its effects. These effects, it turns out, can be predicted with extreme accuracy if specific conditions are identified—in other words, there are laws that can describe the behavior of objects under the influence of gravity. First, the force exerted by gravitation can be described as the product of an object's mass multiplied by its acceleration. This is known as Newton's Second Law of Motion. Moreover, Newton's Law of Universal Gravitation specifies that the force of gravity experienced by two objects is proportional to the product of their masses and inversely proportional to the square of the distance between them. In other words, if one specifies the masses of two objects and their distance from one another, one can calculate with great precision the force of gravity to which they will be subject and how they will behave as a consequence. Deviations from the expected orbit of Uranus based on physical laws allowed the existence and location of another massive object to be predicted—the object in question, the planet Neptune, was discovered in 1846 within 1° of its inferred position.

Of course, acknowledging, describing, or even predicting the effects of gravity do not explain how the phenomenon works or why it has the properties that it does. Facts and laws are insufficient for a deeper understanding of gravitation; to achieve this requires a testable, substantiated, comprehensive explanation that is consistent with all known facts about gravity—in other words, a theory. Many theories of gravitation have been proposed, and most of them have failed tests or have been inconsistent with accepted facts and have therefore been rejected. The reigning theory, Einstein's Theory of General Relativity, explains gravity as the consequence of the warping of space–time, the fabric of the universe, by mass. Einstein's theory has triumphed to date because it has been able to account for observations that other theories (e.g., Newton's) could not, such as the characteristics of the orbit of Mercury and the bending of light by mass. In fact, it was a test of the latter, during an eclipse in 1919, that made Einstein an international celebrity.

Relativity, like any other theory in science, continues to be tested. Notably, Kramer et al. (2006) recently highlighted the utility of a double pulsar system in space as "a good candidate for testing Einstein's theory of general relativity and alternative theories of gravity." The fact that global positioning satellite (GPS) systems would not work without correcting for the implications of relativity represents an indirect confirmation as well.

Einstein's theory is not complete, however. For one, it has not been possible thus far to reconcile relativity with observations (rather, inferences) about the nature of the universe at the subatomic scales at which quantum processes operate. It also does not explain why gravity is such a weak force relative to the other known forces (electromagnetism and the strong and weak nuclear forces). Indeed, a trivial application of electromagnetic force is more than sufficient to counteract the force of gravity exerted by the entire planet, as when a paperclip is lifted with a small magnet. Explaining these properties of gravity remains an active area of research in theoretical physics (Randall 2005).

## Evolution as Fact

The notion that species may change through time and that living organisms are related to one another through common descent was not original to Charles Darwin. Ideas regarding evolutionary change, as with ideas about gravity, extend back at least to a few ancient Greek thinkers. There

had been much discussion of this topic two generations before Darwin based on the writings of Jean-Baptiste de Lamarck, and Darwin's own grandfather, Erasmus Darwin, was explicit in his view that species could change. Darwin's major contribution on this issue was not to introduce the idea, but to assemble a massive compendium of data in support of what he called "descent with modification."

In *The Origin of Species*, published in 1859, Darwin cited independent lines of evidence such as the biogeographical distribution of species, homology of structure, the occurrence of vestigial organs and atavisms, and the already well-established process of extinction as all pointing to a conclusion that species have changed over time and are connected by descent from common ancestors. Through the force of Darwin's argument and the mass of supporting data he presented, it was not long before the contemporary scientific community came to acknowledge the historical reality of evolutionary descent. As A.W. Bennett summarized the situation in 1870,

> The fascinating hypothesis of [descent with modification] has, within the last few years, so completely taken hold of the scientific mind, both in [Great Britain] and in Germany, that almost the whole of our rising men of science may be classed as belonging to this school of thought. Probably since the time of Newton no man has had so great an influence over the development of scientific thought as Mr. Darwin.

Over the past 150 years, this initial list has been supplemented by countless observations in paleontology, comparative anatomy, developmental biology, molecular biology, and (most recently) comparative genomics, and through direct observations of evolutionary change in both natural and experimental populations. Each of thousands of peer-reviewed articles published every year in scientific journals provides further confirmation (though, as Futuyma (1998) notes, "no biologist today would think of publishing a paper on 'new evidence for evolution'...it simply hasn't been an issue in scientific circles for more than a century"). Conversely, no reliable observation has ever been found to contradict the general notion of common descent. It should come as no surprise, then, that the scientific community at large has accepted evolutionary descent as a historical reality since Darwin's time and considers it among the most reliably established and fundamentally important facts in all of science.

## Evolution as Theory

Establishing the fact of evolution was only half of Darwin's objective. He also sought to explain this fact by proposing a mechanism: his Theory of Evolution by Natural Selection. As he stated in 1871, "I had two distinct objects in view; firstly, to show that species had not been separately created, and secondly, that natural selection had been the chief agent of change."

Natural selection was neither the first nor the last theory proposed to explain the fact of evolution. Lamarck's theory, in particular, had been based on two key ideas: "use and disuse" and the inheritance of acquired characteristics. In combination, these suggested that the traits acquired through use by organisms during their lifetimes would be passed on to offspring (for example, that the children of individuals who exercise vigorously would be born with greater musculature) and conversely that features that went unused would be lost. (The notion that evolutionary change occurs in response to need in combination with an internal striving toward greater perfection is a common misconception that is often attributed to Lamarck; see Kampourakis and Zogza 2007 for criticism of this practice). Lamarck's proposed mechanism is not compatible with the modern understanding of genetics and has therefore been abandoned. However, it seems that it and the notion of striving to fulfill needs are more intuitive than Darwinian natural selection,[1] which probably explains why they were proposed first and why so many students and others continue to conceive of evolution in these inaccurate terms (Bishop and Anderson 1990; Demastes et al. 1995; Alters and Nelson 2002). A similar phenomenon has been observed in physics education, in which Newtonian or Einsteinian ideas taught to students must compete with incorrect but evidently more intuitive Aristotelian preconceptions (Halloun and Hestenes 1985a,b).

Although he succeeded in establishing the fact of evolution in short order, Darwin did not live to see natural selection adopted as a central mechanism in evolutionary theory. In fact, by the dawn of the 20th century, natural selection had been nearly eclipsed as a favored mechanism of evolutionary change. Theories involving instantaneous, rather than gradual, changes (mutationism), internal forces creating a sort of unavoidable evolutionary inertia even to the point of extinction (orthogenesis), and renewed appeals to use and disuse (neo-Lamarckism) had moved into the spotlight (Bowler 1992). It was not until the "Modern Synthesis" of the 1930s and 1940s that natural selection returned to the fore when it was shown to be compatible with Mendel's laws of inheritance[2] (Mayr and Provine 1980; Bowler 2003). Darwin himself had no knowledge of genetics, making this revised version sufficiently distinct from the original to qualify as "neo-Darwinian theory."

Modern evolutionary theory represents a multifaceted set of explanations for patterns observed both in contemporary populations and in deep time as revealed by the fossil record. Natural selection is considered by many to be the prime component of evolutionary theory and is the only workable mechanism ever proposed that is capable of accounting for the adaptive features of organisms. At the molecular level, nonadaptive mechanisms are recognized as highly significant, and there is also an increasing emphasis on changes due to processes such as genetic drift that differ from natural selection by being due to chance.[3]

---

1. The components of evolutionary biology dealing specifically with natural selection are "Darwinian" (as opposed to, say, "Lamarckian" mechanisms). Similarly, descriptions of gravity can legitimately be considered "Newtonian" or "Einsteinian" depending on which theory is being invoked. By contrast, the labels "Darwinism" for an acceptance of the fact of evolution and "Darwinists" for those who acknowledge common descent as a historical reality are used primarily as a pejorative description by antievolutionists. It is roughly equivalent to using a moniker such as "Newtonism" to describe the acceptance of the physical reality of gravity or "Einsteinists" for those who acknowledge gravity to be a fact. Scientists who study evolution are properly known as "evolutionary biologists" or sometimes "evolutionists."

2. Being scientific laws, these describe the outcome of a system under defined conditions, specifically, the way that genes are inherited by offspring in organisms with sexual reproduction and two copies of the chromosome set (diploids), in the absence of any complicating factors.

3. Genetic drift involves changes in the genetic composition of populations due to chance events and is most powerful in small populations. It is also widely recognized that mutations, which are the source of the genetic variation upon which other evolutionary processes depend, is "random" in the sense that mutations occur without regard to their consequences for organisms, although not all are equally likely. Natural selection, on the other hand, is the *opposite of random chance*. While there are chance elements involved (mutation and genetic drift), it is a deep misconception to equate evolution as a whole to random chance.

Because of this complexity, biologists rarely make reference to "the theory of evolution," referring instead simply to "evolution" (i.e., the fact of descent with modification) or "evolutionary theory" (i.e., the increasingly sophisticated body of explanations for the fact of evolution). That evolution is a theory in the proper scientific sense means that there is both a fact of evolution to be explained and a well-supported mechanistic framework to account for it. To claim that evolution is "just a theory" is to reveal both a profound ignorance of modern biological knowledge and a deep misunderstanding of the basic nature of science.

## Evolution as Path

Some scientific disciplines—geology, archeology, astronomy, and evolutionary biology among them—deal not only with general processes and mechanisms, but also unique historical particulars. In addition to its incarnations as a "fact" and a "theory," evolution also can be discussed in a third distinct capacity, namely, as a "path" (Ruse 1997). Evolution as path deals with the factual details of life's history, such as the degree of relatedness of modern species to one another, the timing of splits among lineages, the characteristics of extinct ancestors, and the major events that have occurred over the nearly 4 billion years of life's saga. As an example, specialists including paleontologists and molecular systematists may investigate whether birds are the descendants of a lineage of dinosaurs (and if so, which one), when flight first evolved and what changes this entailed, and what the patterns of diversification of birds have been since the evolution of flight. Similar questions can be asked about each branch of the tree of life.

As Moran (1993) noted, some details of life's history are insufficiently established to warrant designation as "facts," but this can (and probably will) change as more data are brought to bear on particular issues. For example, it is now an accepted fact that dinosaurs were the dominant terrestrial vertebrates for a period of 160 million years and that they disappeared comparatively abruptly about 65 million years ago. It is not yet clear, however, what the implications of this mass extinction event were for the subsequent evolution of the mammals and birds who now fill many of the niches previously occupied by dinosaurs (Bininda-Emonds et al. 2007; Wible et al. 2007).

As with its status as scientific fact and its nature as theory, there are often confusions about the path of evolution among nonspecialists. The erroneous notion that humans descended from chimpanzees or monkeys falls into this category. Chimps and humans are not related as ancestors and descendants, but rather as cousins whose lineages last shared a common ancestor about 6 million years ago. A great deal of change has occurred along both lineages since their split from this common ancestor, and many species have come and gone along both lines of descent.

## Debates About Theory and Path Do Not Impinge on Fact

Evolutionary biology has as its purview the entire history and diversity of life, encompassing an unbroken chain of ancestry and descent involving innumerable organisms and spanning billions of years. In light of the tremendous scope and complexity of its subject matter, it should come as no surprise that details regarding the path and mechanisms of evolution are often subject to heated debate. The fact of evolution, however, remains unsinged. To quote Gould (1981) once again,

> Scientists regard debates on fundamental issues of theory as a sign of intellectual health and a source of excitement. Science is—and how else can I say it?—most fun when it plays with interesting ideas, examines their implications, and recognizes that old information might be explained in surprisingly new ways. Evolutionary theory is now enjoying this uncommon vigor. Yet amidst all this turmoil no biologist has been led to doubt the fact that evolution occurred; we are debating how it happened.

Is evolution always gradual, or can it follow a more punctuated pattern? Are chance mechanisms such as genetic drift ever as important as the nonrandom process of natural selection? Does natural selection operate only among organisms (or genes) within populations, or can it occur at other levels such as among groups or species? Did mammals diversify as a consequence of the extinction of dinosaurs? Is the primary divide among groups of organisms between those with and those without nuclei, or are there deeper splits? Are wholescale genome duplications common in evolution, and if so, are they associated with major evolutionary changes? Can complex features ever be regained once they have been lost from a lineage? Is a substantial fraction of noncoding DNA functional, or is most of it simply "junk" or "parasitic"? Was *Australopithecus afarensis* ("Lucy") a direct ancestor of *Homo sapiens* or a member of a different hominid lineage? Debate over these questions of theory and path can become quite acrimonious within evolutionary biology, but in no case do they raise doubt about the fact of evolution. As Gould (1981) noted, "facts do not go away when scientists debate rival theories to explain them."

In broader terms, evidence for a given fact can be accepted at the same time that a proposed explanation for it is rejected—this is, after all, precisely what happened in Darwin's case as mutationism, orthogenesis, and neo-Lamarckism competed with natural selection before the rise of the Modern Synthesis. Responding to critics in 1871, Darwin wrote:

> Some of those who admit the principle of evolution, but reject natural selection, seem to forget, when criticising my book, that I had the above two objects in view; hence if I have erred in giving to natural selection great power, which I am very far from admitting, or in having exaggerated its power, which is in itself probable, I have at least, as I hope, done good service in aiding to overthrow the dogma of separate creations.

Indeed, Darwin was very explicit about the distinction between descent with modification (fact) and natural selection (theory). As he noted in 1863:

> Whether the naturalist believes in the views given by Lamarck, or Geoffroy St.-Hilaire, by the author of the 'Vestiges,' by Mr. Wallace and myself, or in any other such view, signifies extremely little in comparison with the admission that species have descended from other species and have not been created immutable; for he who admits this as a great truth has a wide field opened to him for further inquiry.

Unfortunately, conflation of fact and theory in this regard is not limited to opponents of evolution. Some biologists make the inverse mistake of considering clear evidence of common descent as evidence that it occurred by natural selection. Certainly, one can propose that natural selection is responsible for any changes that show evidence of having been adaptive, but change through time (evolution as fact or path) does not, by itself, evince any particular mechanism (evolution as theory). Neither this failure to distinguish between fact or path and theory by scientists,

nor that perpetuated by antievolutionists, is compatible with a proper understanding of the scientific definitions of these terms.

## Concluding Remarks

It has been noted many times that evolution is both a fact and a theory (Gould 1981; Moran 1993; Futuyma 1998; Lenski 2000). It can also be considered in terms of a historical path (Ruse 1997). The fact of evolution, that organisms alive today are related by descent from common ancestors, is fundamental to an understanding of biology. As Dobzhansky (1973) famously stated, "nothing in biology makes sense except in the light of evolution." Nevertheless, a great deal remains to be determined regarding the mechanisms that have created (and destroyed) biological diversity since the emergence of life on Earth. Put in another way, modern evolutionary biology rests upon an extraordinarily solid foundation supported by multiple pillars of evidence, while its theoretical framework remains under construction. That the edifice of evolutionary theory is not yet complete is no cause for concern. Indeed, this is what makes evolutionary biology such an exciting and dynamic modern science.

"Evolution as Fact, Theory and Path," T. Ryan Gregory, EVOLUTION: EDUCATION AND OUTREACH, 2008, 1:46–52. Reprinted with permission from Springer, obtained via RightsLink.

# 3 EVOLUTION AND THE ORIGINS OF DISEASE

**Randolph M. Nesse and George C. Williams**

*The principles of evolution by natural selection
are finally beginning to inform medicine*

Thoughtful contemplation of the human body elicits awe—in equal measure with perplexity. The eye, for instance, has long been an object of wonder, with the clear, living tissue of the cornea curving just the right amount, the iris adjusting to brightness and the lens to distance, so that the optimal quantity of light focuses exactly on the surface of the retina. Admiration of such apparent perfection soon gives way, however, to consternation. Contrary to any sensible design, blood vessels and nerves traverse the inside of the retina, creating a blind spot at their point of exit.

The body is a bundle of such jarring contradictions. For each exquisite heart valve, we have a wisdom tooth. Strands of DNA direct the development of the 10 trillion cells that make up a human adult but then permit his or her steady deterioration and eventual death. Our immune system can identify and destroy a million kinds of foreign matter, yet many bacteria can still kill us. These contradictions make it appear as if the body was designed by a team of superb engineers with occasional interventions by Rube Goldberg.

In fact, such seeming incongruities make sense but only when we investigate the origins of the body's vulnerabilities while keeping in mind the wise words of distinguished geneticist Theodosius Dobzhansky: "Nothing in biology makes sense except in the light of evolution." Evolutionary biology is, of course, the scientific foundation for all biology, and biology is the foundation for all medicine. To a surprising degree, however, evolutionary biology is just now being recognized as a basic medical science. The enterprise of studying medical problems in an evolutionary context has been termed Darwinian medicine. Most medical research tries to explain the causes of an individual's disease and seeks therapies to cure or relieve deleterious conditions. These efforts are traditionally based on consideration of proximate issues, the straightforward study of the body's anatomic and physiological mechanisms as they currently exist. In contrast, Darwinian medicine asks why the body is designed in a way that makes us all vulnerable to problems like cancer, atherosclerosis, depression and choking, thus offering a broader context in which to conduct research.

The evolutionary explanations for the body's flaws fall into surprisingly few categories. First, some discomforting conditions, such as pain, fever, cough, vomiting and anxiety, are actually neither diseases nor design defects but rather are evolved defenses. Second, conflicts with other organisms—*Escherichia coli* or crocodiles, for instance—are a fact of life. Third, some circumstances, such as the ready availability of dietary fats, are so recent that natural selection has not yet had a chance to deal with them. Fourth, the body may fall victim to tradeoffs between a trait's benefits and its costs; a textbook example is the sickle cell gene, which also protects against malaria. Finally, the process of natural selection is constrained in ways that leave us with suboptimal design features, as in the case of the mammalian eye.

### Evolved Defenses

Perhaps the most obviously useful defense mechanism is coughing; people who cannot clear foreign matter from their lungs are likely to die from pneumonia. The capacity for pain is also certainly beneficial. The rare individuals who cannot feel pain fail even to experience discomfort from staying in the same position for long periods. Their unnatural stillness impairs the blood supply to their joints, which then deteriorate. Such pain-free people usually die by early adulthood from tissue damage and infections. Cough or pain is usually interpreted as disease or trauma but is actually part of the solution rather than the problem. These defensive capabilities, shaped by natural selection, are kept in reserve until needed.

Less widely recognized as defenses are fever, nausea, vomiting, diarrhea, anxiety, fatigue, sneezing and inflammation. Even some physicians remain unaware of fever's utility. No mere increase in metabolic rate, fever is a carefully regulated rise in the set point of the body's thermostat. The higher body temperature facilitates the destruction of pathogens. Work by Matthew J. Kluger of the Lovelace Institute in Albuquerque, N.M., has shown that even cold-blooded lizards, when infected, move to warmer places until their bodies are several degrees above their usual temperature. If prevented from moving to the warm

part of their cage, they are at increased risk of death from the infection. In a similar study by Evelyn Satinoff of the University of Delaware, elderly rats, who can no longer achieve the high fevers of their younger lab companions, also instinctively sought hotter environments when challenged by infection.

A reduced level of iron in the blood is another misunderstood defense mechanism. People suffering from chronic infection often have decreased levels of blood iron. Although such low iron is sometimes blamed for the illness, it actually is a protective response: during infection, iron is sequestered in the liver, which prevents invading bacteria from getting adequate supplies of this vital element.

Morning sickness has long been considered an unfortunate side effect of pregnancy. The nausea, however, coincides with the period of rapid tissue differentiation of the fetus, when development is most vulnerable to interference by toxins. And nauseated women tend to restrict their intake of strong-tasting, potentially harmful substances. These observations led independent researcher Margie Profet to hypothesize that the nausea of pregnancy is an adaptation whereby the mother protects the fetus from exposure to toxins. Profet tested this idea by examining pregnancy outcomes. Sure enough, women with more nausea were less likely to suffer miscarriages. (This evidence supports the hypothesis but is hardly conclusive. If Profet is correct, further research should discover that pregnant females of many species show changes in food preferences. Her theory also predicts an increase in birth defects among offspring of women who have little or no morning sickness and thus eat a wider variety of foods during pregnancy.)

Another common condition, anxiety, obviously originated as a defense in dangerous situations by promoting escape and avoidance. A 1992 study by Lee A. Dugatkin of the University of Louisville evaluated the benefits of fear in guppies. He grouped them as timid, ordinary or bold, depending on their reaction to the presence of smallmouth bass. The timid hid, the ordinary simply swam away, and the bold maintained their ground and eyed the bass. Each guppy group was then left alone in a tank with a bass. After 60 hours, 40 percent of the timid guppies had survived, as had only 15 percent of the ordinary fish. The entire complement of bold guppies, on the other hand, wound up aiding the transmission of bass genes rather than their own.

Selection for genes promoting anxious behaviors implies that there should be people who experience too much anxiety, and indeed there are. There should also be hypophobic individuals who have insufficient anxiety, either because of genetic tendencies or antianxiety drugs. The exact nature and frequency of such a syndrome is an open question, as few people come to psychiatrists complaining of insufficient apprehension. But if sought, the pathologically nonanxious may be found in emergency rooms, jails and unemployment lines.

The utility of common and unpleasant conditions such as diarrhea, fever and anxiety is not intuitive. If natural selection shapes the mechanisms that regulate defensive responses, how can people get away with using drugs to block these defenses without doing their bodies obvious harm? Part of the answer is that we do, in fact, sometimes do ourselves a disservice by disrupting defenses.

Herbert L. DuPont of the University of Texas at Houston and Richard B. Hornick of Orlando Regional Medical Center studied the diarrhea caused by *Shigella* infection and found that people who took anti-diarrhea drugs stayed sick longer and were more likely to have complications than those who took a placebo. In another example, Eugene D. Weinberg of Indiana University has documented that well-intentioned attempts to correct perceived iron deficiencies have led to increases in infectious disease, especially amebiasis, in parts of Africa. Although the iron in most oral supplements is unlikely to make much difference in otherwise healthy people with everyday infections, it can severely harm those who are infected and malnourished. Such people cannot make enough protein to bind the iron, leaving it free for use by infectious agents.

On the morning-sickness front, an antinausea drug was recently blamed for birth defects. It appears that no consideration was given to the possibility that the drug itself might be harmless to the fetus but could still be associated with birth defects, by interfering with the mother's defensive nausea.

Another obstacle to perceiving the benefits of defenses arises from the observation that many individuals regularly experience seemingly worthless reactions of anxiety, pain, fever, diarrhea or nausea. The explanation requires an analysis of the regulation of defensive responses in terms of signal-detection theory. A circulating toxin may come from something in the stomach. An organism can expel it by vomiting, but only at a price. The cost of a false alarm—vomiting when no toxin is truly present—is only a few calories. But the penalty for a single missed authentic alarm—failure to vomit when confronted with a toxin—may be death.

Natural selection therefore tends to shape regulation mechanisms with hair triggers, following what we call the smoke-detector principle. A smoke alarm that will reliably wake a sleeping family in the event of any fire will necessarily give a false alarm every time the toast burns. The price of the human body's numerous "smoke alarms" is much suffering that is completely normal but in most instances unnecessary. This principle also explains why blocking defenses is so often free of tragic consequences. Because most defensive reactions occur in response to insignificant threats, interference is usually harmless; the vast majority of alarms that are stopped by removing the battery from the smoke alarm are false ones, so this strategy may seem reasonable. Until, that is, a real fire occurs.

### Conflicts with Other Organisms

Natural selection is unable to provide us with perfect protection against all pathogens, because they tend to evolve much faster than humans do. *E. coli*, for example, with its rapid rates of reproduction, has as much opportunity for mutation and selection in one day as humanity gets in a millennium. And our defenses, whether natural or artificial, make for potent selection forces. Pathogens either quickly evolve a counterdefense or become extinct. Amherst College biologist Paul W. Ewald has suggested classifying phenomena associated with infection according to whether they benefit the host, the pathogen, both or neither. Consider the runny nose associated with a cold. Nasal mucous secretion could expel intruders, speed the pathogen's transmission to new hosts or both [see "The Evolution of Virulence," by Paul W. Ewald; Scientific American, April 1993]. Answers could come from studies examining whether blocking nasal secretions shortens or prolongs illness, but few such studies have been done.

Humanity won huge battles in the war against pathogens with the development of antibiotics and vaccines. Our victories were so rapid and seemingly complete that in 1969 U.S. Surgeon General William H. Stewart said that it was "time to close the book on infectious disease." But the enemy, and the power of natural selection, had been underestimated. The sober reality is that pathogens apparently can adapt to every chemical researchers develop. ("The war has been won," one scientist more recently quipped. "By the other side.")

Antibiotic resistance is a classic demonstration of natural selection. Bacteria that happen to have genes that allow them to prosper despite the presence of an antibiotic reproduce faster than others, and so the genes that confer resistance spread quickly. As shown by Nobel laureate Joshua Lederberg of the Rockefeller University, they can even jump to different species of bacteria, borne on bits of infectious DNA. Today some strains of tuberculosis in New York City are resistant to all three main antibiotic treatments; patients with those strains have no better chance of surviving than did TB patients a century ago. Stephen S. Morse of Columbia University notes that the multidrug-resistant strain that has spread throughout the East Coast may have originated in a homeless shelter across the street from Columbia-Presbyterian Medical Center. Such a phenomenon would indeed be predicted in an environment where fierce selection pressure quickly weeds out less hardy strains. The surviving bacilli have been bred for resistance.

Many people, including some physicians and scientists, still believe the outdated theory that pathogens necessarily become benign after long association with hosts. Superficially, this makes sense. An organism that kills rapidly may never get to a new host, so natural selection would seem to favor lower virulence. Syphilis, for instance, was a highly virulent disease when it first arrived in Europe, but as the centuries passed it became steadily more mild. The virulence of a pathogen is, however, a life history trait that can increase as well as decrease, depending on which option is more advantageous to its genes.

For agents of disease that are spread directly from person to person, low virulence tends to be beneficial, as it allows the host to remain active and in contact with other potential hosts. But some diseases, like malaria, are transmitted just as well—or better—by the incapacitated. For such pathogens, which usually rely on intermediate vectors like mosquitoes, high virulence can give a selective advantage. This principle has direct implications for infection control in hospitals, where health care workers' hands can be vectors that lead to selection for more virulent strains.

In the case of cholera, public water supplies play the mosquitoes' role. When water for drinking and bathing is contaminated by waste from immobilized patients, selection tends to increase virulence, because more diarrhea enhances the spread of the organism even if individual hosts quickly die. But, as Ewald has shown, when sanitation improves, selection acts against classical *Vibrio cholerae* bacteria in favor of the more benign El Tor biotype. Under these conditions, a dead host is a dead end. But a less ill and more mobile host, able to infect many others over a much longer time, is an effective vehicle for a pathogen of lower virulence. In another example, better sanitation leads to displacement of the aggressive *Shigella flexneri* by the more benign *S. sonnei*.

Such considerations may be relevant for public policy. Evolutionary theory predicts that clean needles and the encouragement of safe sex will do more than save numerous individuals from HIV infection. If humanity's behavior itself slows HIV transmission rates, strains that do not soon kill their hosts have the long-term survival advantage over the more virulent viruses that then die with their hosts, denied the opportunity to spread. Our collective choices can change the very nature of HIV.

Conflicts with other organisms are not limited to pathogens. In times past, humans were at great risk from predators looking for a meal. Except in a few places, large carnivores now pose no threat to humans. People are in more danger today from smaller organisms' defenses, such as the venoms of spiders and snakes. Ironically, our fears of small creatures, in the form of phobias, probably cause more harm than any interactions with those organisms do. Far more dangerous than predators or poisoners are other members of our own species. We attack each other not to get meat but to get mates, territory and other resources. Violent conflicts between individuals are overwhelmingly between young men in competition and give rise to organizations to advance these aims. Armies, again usually composed of young men, serve similar objectives, at huge cost.

Even the most intimate human relationships give rise to conflicts having medical implications. The reproductive interests of a mother and her infant, for instance, may seem congruent at first but soon diverge. As noted by biologist Robert L. Trivers in a now classic 1974 paper, when her child is a few years old, the mother's genetic interests may be best served by becoming pregnant again, whereas her offspring benefits from continuing to nurse. Even in the womb there is contention. From the mother's vantage point, the optimal size of a fetus is a bit smaller than that which would best serve the fetus and the father. This discord, according to David Haig of Harvard University, gives rise to an arms race between fetus and mother over her levels of blood pressure and blood sugar, sometimes resulting in hypertension and diabetes during pregnancy.

### Coping with Novelty

Making rounds in any modern hospital provides sad testimony to the prevalence of diseases humanity has brought on itself. Heart attacks, for example, result mainly from atherosclerosis, a problem that became widespread only in this century and that remains rare among hunter-gatherers. Epidemiological research furnishes the information that should help us prevent heart attacks: limit fat intake, eat lots of vegetables, and exercise hard each day. But hamburger chains proliferate, diet foods languish on the shelves, and exercise machines serve as expensive clothing hangers throughout the land. The proportion of overweight Americans is one third and rising. We all know what is good for us. Why do so many of us continue to make unhealthy choices?

Our poor decisions about diet and exercise are made by brains shaped to cope with an environment substantially different from the one our species now inhabits. On the African savanna, where the modern human design was fine-tuned, fat, salt and sugar were scarce and precious. Individuals who had a tendency to consume large amounts of fat when given the rare opportunity had a selective advantage. They were more likely to survive famines that killed their thinner companions. And we, their descendants, still carry those urges for foodstuffs that today are anything but scarce. These evolved desires—inflamed by advertisements from competing food corporations that themselves survive by selling us more of whatever we want to buy—easily defeat our intellect and willpower. How ironic that humanity worked for centuries to create environments that are almost literally flowing with milk and honey, only to see our success responsible for much modern disease and untimely death.

Increasingly, people also have easy access to many kinds of drugs, especially alcohol and tobacco, that are responsible for a huge proportion of disease, health care costs and premature death. Although individuals have always used

psychoactive substances, widespread problems materialized only following another environmental novelty: the ready availability of concentrated drugs and new, direct routes of administration, especially injection. Most of these substances, including nicotine, cocaine and opium, are products of natural selection that evolved to protect plants from insects. Because humans share a common evolutionary heritage with insects, many of these substances also affect our nervous system.

This perspective suggests that it is not just defective individuals or disordered societies that are vulnerable to the dangers of psychoactive drugs; all of us are susceptible because drugs and our biochemistry have a long history of interaction. Understanding the details of that interaction, which is the focus of much current research from both a proximate and evolutionary perspective, may well lead to better treatments for addiction.

The relatively recent and rapid increase in breast cancer must be the result in large part of changing environments and ways of life, with only a few cases resulting solely from genetic abnormalities. Boyd Eaton and his colleagues at Emory University reported that the rate of breast cancer in today's "nonmodern" societies is only a tiny fraction of that in the U.S. They hypothesize that the amount of time between menarche and first pregnancy is a crucial risk factor, as is the related issue of total lifetime number of menstrual cycles. In hunter-gatherers, menarche occurs at about age 15 or later, followed within a few years by pregnancy and two or three years of nursing, then by another pregnancy soon after. Only between the end of nursing and the next pregnancy will the woman menstruate and thus experience the high levels of hormones that may adversely affect breast cells.

In modern societies, in contrast, menarche occurs at age 12 or 13—probably at least in part because of a fat intake sufficient to allow an extremely young woman to nourish a fetus—and the first pregnancy may be decades later or never. A female hunter-gatherer may have a total of 150 menstrual cycles, whereas the average woman in modern societies has 400 or more. Although few would suggest that women should become pregnant in their teens to prevent breast cancer later, early administration of a burst of hormones to simulate pregnancy may reduce the risk. Trials to test this idea are now under way at the University of California at San Diego.

### Trade-Offs and Constraints

Compromise is inherent in every adaptation. Arm bones three times their current thickness would almost never break, but *Homo sapiens* would be lumbering creatures on a never-ending quest for calcium. More sensitive ears might sometimes be useful, but we would be distracted by the noise of air molecules banging into our eardrums.

Such trade-offs also exist at the genetic level. If a mutation offers a net reproductive advantage, it will tend to increase in frequency in a population even if it causes vulnerability to disease. People with two copies of the sickle cell gene, for example, suffer terrible pain and die young. People with two copies of the "normal" gene are at high risk of death from malaria. But individuals with one of each are protected from both malaria and sickle cell disease. Where malaria is prevalent, such people are fitter, in the Darwinian sense, than members of either other group. So even though the sickle cell gene causes disease, it is selected for where malaria persists. Which is the "healthy" allele in this environment? The question has no answer. There is no one normal human genome—there are only genes.

Many other genes that cause disease must also have offered benefits, at least in some environments, or they would not be so common. Because cystic fibrosis (CF) kills one out of 2,500 Caucasians, the responsible genes would appear to be at great risk of being eliminated from the gene pool. And yet they endure. For years, researchers mused that the CF gene, like the sickle cell gene, probably conferred some advantage. Recently a study by Gerald B. Pier of Harvard Medical School and his colleagues gave substance to this informed speculation: having one copy of the CF gene appears to decrease the chances of the bearer acquiring a typhoid fever infection, which once had a 15 percent mortality.

Aging may be the ultimate example of a genetic trade-off. In 1957 one of us (Williams) suggested that genes that cause aging and eventual death could nonetheless be selected for if they had other effects that gave an advantage in youth, when the force of selection is stronger. For instance, a hypothetical gene that governs calcium metabolism so that bones heal quickly but that also happens to cause the steady deposition of calcium in arterial walls might well be selected for even though it kills some older people. The influence of such pleiotropic genes (those having multiple effects) has been seen in fruit flies and flour beetles, but no specific example has yet been found in humans. Gout, however, is of particular interest, because it arises when a potent antioxidant, uric acid, forms crystals that precipitate out of fluid in joints. Antioxidants have antiaging effects, and plasma levels of uric acid in different species of primates are closely correlated with average adult life span. Perhaps high levels of uric acid benefit most humans by slowing tissue aging, while a few pay the price with gout.

Other examples are more likely to contribute to more rapid aging. For instance, strong immune defenses protect us from infection but also inflict continuous, low-level tissue damage. It is also possible, of course, that most genes that cause aging have no benefit at any age—they simply never decreased reproductive fitness enough in the natural environment to be selected against. Nevertheless, over the next decade research will surely identify specific genes that accelerate senescence, and researchers will soon thereafter gain the means to interfere with their actions or even change them. Before we tinker, however, we should determine whether these actions have benefits early in life.

Because evolution can take place only in the direction of time's arrow, an organism's design is constrained by structures already in place. As noted, the vertebrate eye is arranged backward. The squid eye, in contrast, is free from this defect, with vessels and nerves running on the outside, penetrating where necessary and pinning down the retina so it cannot detach. The human eye's flaw results from simple bad luck; hundreds of millions of years ago, the layer of cells that happened to become sensitive to light in our ancestors was positioned differently from the corresponding layer in ancestors of squids. The two designs evolved along separate tracks, and there is no going back.

Such path dependence also explains why the simple act of swallowing can be life-threatening. Our respiratory and food passages intersect because in an early lungfish ancestor the air opening for breathing at the surface was understandably located at the top of the snout and led into a common space shared by the food passageway. Because natural selection cannot start from scratch, humans are stuck with the possibility that food will clog the opening to our lungs.

The path of natural selection can even lead to a potentially fatal cul-de-sac, as in the case of the appendix, that vestige of a cavity that our ancestors employed in digestion. Because it no longer performs that function, and as it can kill when infected, the expectation might be that natural selection would have eliminated it. The reality is more complex. Appendicitis results when inflammation causes swelling, which compresses the artery supplying blood to the appendix. Blood flow protects against bacterial growth, so any reduction aids infection, which creates more swelling. If the blood supply is cut off completely, bacteria have free rein until the appendix bursts. A slender appendix is especially susceptible to this chain of events, so appendicitis may, paradoxically, apply the selective pressure that maintains a large appendix. Far from arguing that everything in the body is perfect, an evolutionary analysis reveals that we live with some very unfortunate legacies and that some vulnerabilities may even be actively maintained by the force of natural selection.

### Evolution of Darwinian Medicine

Despite the power of the Darwinian paradigm, evolutionary biology is just now being recognized as a basic science essential for medicine. Most diseases decrease fitness, so it would seem that natural selection could explain only health, not disease. A Darwinian approach makes sense only when the object of explanation is changed from diseases to the traits that make us vulnerable to diseases. The assumption that natural selection maximizes health also is incorrect—selection maximizes the reproductive success of genes. Those genes that make bodies having superior reproductive success will become more common, even if they compromise the individual's health in the end.

Finally, history and misunderstanding have presented obstacles to the acceptance of Darwinian medicine. An evolutionary approach to functional analysis can appear akin to naive teleology or vitalism, errors banished only recently, and with great effort, from medical thinking. And, of course, whenever evolution and medicine are mentioned together, the specter of eugenics arises. Discoveries made through a Darwinian view of how all human bodies are alike in their vulnerability to disease will offer great benefits for individuals, but such insights do not imply that we can or should make any attempt to improve the species. If anything, this approach cautions that apparent genetic defects may have unrecognized adaptive significance, that a single "normal" genome is nonexistent and that notions of "normality" tend to be simplistic.

The systematic application of evolutionary biology to medicine is a new enterprise. Like biochemistry at the beginning of this century, Darwinian medicine very likely will need to develop in several incubators before it can prove its power and utility. If it must progress only from the work of scholars without funding to gather data to test their ideas, it will take decades for the field to mature. Departments of evolutionary biology in medical schools would accelerate the process, but for the most part they do not yet exist. If funding agencies had review panels with evolutionary expertise, research would develop faster, but such panels remain to be created. We expect that they will.

The evolutionary viewpoint provides a deep connection between the states of disease and normal functioning and can integrate disparate avenues of medical research as well as suggest fresh and important areas of inquiry. Its utility and power will ultimately lead to recognition of evolutionary biology as a basic medical science.

# 4 BLACK, WHITE, OTHER:
## Racial Categories Are Cultural Constructs Masquerading as Biology

**Jonathan Marks**

While reading the Sunday edition of *The New York Times* one morning last February, my attention was drawn by an editorial inconsistency. The article I was reading was written by attorney Lani Guinier. (Guinier, you may remember, had been President Clinton's nominee to head the civil rights division at the Department of Justice in 1993. Her name was hastily withdrawn amid a blast of criticism over her views on political representation of minorities.) What had distracted me from the main point of the story was a photo caption that described Guinier as being "half-black." In the text of the article, Guinier had described herself simply as "black."

How can a person be black and half black at the same time? In algebraic terms, this would seem to describe a situation where $x = 1/2\ x$, to which the only solution is $x = 0$.

The inconsistency in the *Times* was trivial, but revealing. It encapsulated a long-standing problem in our use of racial categories—namely, a confusion between biological and cultural heredity. When Guinier is described as "half-black," that is a statement of biological ancestry, for one of her two parents is black. And when Guinier describes herself as black, she is using a cultural category, according to which one can either be black or white, but not both.

Race—as the term is commonly used—is inherited, although not in a strictly biological fashion. It is passed down according to a system of folk heredity, an all-or-nothing system that is different from the quantifiable heredity of biology. But the incompatibility of the two notions of race is sometimes starkly evident—as when the state decides that racial differences are so important that interracial marriages must be regulated or outlawed entirely. Miscegenation laws in this country (which stayed on the books in many states through the 1960s) obliged the legal system to define who belonged in what category. The resulting formula stated that anyone with one-eighth or more black ancestry was a "negro." (A similar formula, defining Jews, was promulgated by the Germans in the Nuremberg Laws of the 1930s.)

Applying such formulas led to the biological absurdity that having one black great-grandparent was sufficient to define a person as black, but having seven white great grandparents was insufficient to define a person as white. Here, race and biology are demonstrably at odds. And the problem is not semantic but conceptual, for race is presented as a category of nature.

Human beings come in a wide variety of sizes, shapes, colors, and forms—or, because we are visually oriented primates, it certainly seems that way. We also come in larger packages called populations; and we are said to belong to even larger and more confusing units, which have long been known as races. The history of the study of human variation is to a large extent the pursuit of those human races—the attempt to identify the small number of fundamentally distinct kinds of people on earth.

This scientific goal stretches back two centuries, to Linnaeus, the father of biological systematics, who radically established *Homo sapiens* as one species within a group of animals he called Primates. Linnaeus's system of naming groups within groups logically implied further breakdown. He consequently sought to establish a number of subspecies within *Homo sapiens*. He identified five: four geographical species (from Europe, Asia, Africa, and America) and one grab-bag subspecies called *monstrosus*. This category was dropped by subsequent researchers (as was Linnaeus's use of criteria such as personality and dress to define his subspecies).

While Linnaeus was not the first to divide humans on the basis of the continents on which they lived, he had given the division a scientific stamp. But in attempting to determine the proper number of subspecies, the heirs of Linnaeus always seemed to find different answers, depending upon the criteria they applied. By the mid-twentieth century, scores of anthropologists—led by Harvard's Earnest Hooton—had expended enormous energy on the problem. But these scholars could not convince one another about the precise nature of the fundamental divisions of our species.

Part of the problem—as with the *Times's* identification of Lani Guinier—was that we humans have two constantly intersecting ways of thinking about the divisions among us. On the one hand, we like to think of "race"—as Linnaeus did—as an objective, biological category. In

this sense, being a member of a race is supposed to be the equivalent of being a member of a species or of a phylum—except that race, on the analogy of subspecies, is an even narrower (and presumably more exclusive and precise) biological category.

The other kind of category into which we humans allocate ourselves—when we say "Serb" or "Hutu" or "Jew" or "Chicano" or "Republican" or "Red Sox fan"—is cultural. The label refers to little or nothing in the natural attributes of its members. These members may not live in the same region and may not even know many others like themselves. What they share is neither strictly nature nor strictly community. The groupings are constructions of human social history.

Membership in these *un*biological groupings may mean the difference between life and death, for they are the categories that allow us to be identified (and accepted or vilified) socially. While membership in (or allegiance to) these categories may be assigned or adopted from birth, the differentia that mark members from nonmembers are symbolic and abstract; they serve to distinguish people who cannot be readily distinguished by nature. So important are these symbolic distinctions that some of the strongest animosities are often expressed between very similar-looking peoples. Obvious examples are Bosnian Serbs and Muslims, Irish and English, Huron and Iroquois.

Obvious natural variation is rarely so important as cultural difference. One simply does not hear of a slaughter of the short people at the hands of the tall, the glabrous at the hands of the hairy, the red-haired at the hands of the brown-haired. When we do encounter genocidal violence between different looking peoples, the two groups are invariably socially or culturally distinct as well. Indeed, the tragic frequency of hatred and genocidal violence between biologically indistinguishable peoples implies that biological differences such as skin color are not motivations but, rather, excuses. They allow nature to be invoked to reinforce group identities and antagonisms that would exist without these physical distinctions. But are there any truly "racial" biological distinctions to be found in our species?

Obviously, if you compare two people from different parts of the world (or whose ancestors came from different parts of the world), they will differ physically, but one cannot therefore define three or four or five basically different kinds of people, as a biological notion of race would imply. The anatomical properties that distinguish people—such as pigmentation, eye form, body build—are not clumped in discrete groups, but distributed along geographical gradients, as are nearly all the genetically determined variants detectable in the human gene pool.

These gradients are produced by three forces. Natural selection adapts populations to local circumstances (like climate) and thereby differentiates them from other populations. Genetic drift (random fluctuations in a gene pool) also differentiates populations from one another, but in non-adaptive ways. And gene flow (via intermarriage and other child-producing unions) acts to homogenize neighboring populations.

In practice, the operations of these forces are difficult to discern. A few features, such as body build and the graduated distribution of the sickle cell anemia gene in populations from western Africa, southern Asia, and the Mediterranean can be plausibly related to the effects of selection. Others, such as the graduated distribution of a small deletion in the mitochondrial DNA of some East Asian, Oceanic, and Native American peoples, or the degree of flatness of the face, seem unlikely to be the result of selection and are probably the results of random biohistorical factors. The cause of the distribution of most features, from nose breadth to blood group, is simply unclear.

The overall result of these forces is evident, however. As Johann Friedrich Blumenbach noted in 1775, "you see that all do so run into one another, and that one variety of mankind does so sensibly pass into the other, that you cannot mark out the limits between them." (Posturing as an heir to Linnaeus, he nonetheless attempted to do so.) But from humanity's gradations in appearance, no defined groupings resembling races readily emerge. The racial categories with which we have become so familiar are the result of our imposing arbitrary cultural boundaries in order to partition gradual biological variation.

Unlike graduated biological distinctions, culturally constructed categories are ultrasharp. One can be French or German, but not both; Tutsi or Hutu, but not both; Jew or Catholic, but not both; Bosnian Muslim or Serb, but not both; black or white, but not both. Traditionally, people of "mixed race" have been obliged to choose one and thereby identify themselves unambiguously to census takers and administrative bookkeepers—a practice that is now being widely called into question.

A scientific definition of race would require considerable homogeneity within each group, and reasonably discrete differences between groups, but three kinds of data militate against this view: First, the groups traditionally described as races are not at all homogeneous. Africans and Europeans, for instance, are each a collection of biologically diverse populations. Anthropologists of the 1920s widely recognized *three* European races: Nordic, Alpine, and Mediterranean. This implied that races could exist within races. American anthropologist Carleton Coon identified *ten* European races in 1939. With such protean use, the term race came to have little value in describing actual biological entities within *Homo sapiens*. The scholars were not only grappling with a broad north-south gradient in human appearance across Europe, they were trying to bring the data into line with their belief in profound and fundamental constitutional differences between groups of people.

But there simply isn't one European race to contrast with an African race, nor three, nor ten: the question (as scientists long posed it) fails to recognize the actual patterning of diversity in the human species. Fieldwork revealed, and genetics later quantified, the existence of far more biological diversity within any group than between groups. Fatter and thinner people exist everywhere, as do people with type O and type A blood. What generally varies from one population to the next is the *proportion* of people in these groups expressing the trait or gene. Hair color varies strikingly among Europeans and native Australians, but little among other peoples. To focus on discovering differences between presumptive races, when the vast majority of detectable variants do not help differentiate them, was thus to define a very narrow—if not largely illusory—problem in human biology. (The fact that Africans are biologically more diverse than Europeans, but have rarely been split into so many races, attests to the cultural basis of these categorizations.)

Second, differences between human groups are only evident when contrasting geographical extremes. Noting these extremes, biologists of an earlier era sought to identify representatives of "pure," primordial races presumably located in Norway, Senegal, and Thailand. At no time, however, was our species composed of a few populations within which everyone looked pretty much the same. Ever since some of our ancestors left Africa to spread out through the Old World, we humans have always lived in the "in-between" places. And human populations have also always been in genetic contact with one another. Indeed, for tens of thousands of years, humans have had trade networks; and where goods flow, so do genes. Consequently, we have no basis for considering *extreme* human forms the most pure, or most representative, of some ancient primordial populations. Instead, they represent populations adapted to the most disparate environments.

And third, between each presumptive "major" race are unclassifiable populations and people. Some populations of India, for example, are darkly pigmented (or "black"), have Europeanlike ("Caucasoid") facial features, but inhabit the continent of Asia (which should make them "Asian"). Americans might tend to ignore these "exceptions" to the racial categories, since immigrants to the United States from West Africa, Southeast Asia, and northwest Europe far outnumber those from India. The very existence of unclassifiable peoples undermines the idea that there are just three human biological groups in the Old World. Yet acknowledging the biological distinctiveness of such groups leads to a rapid proliferation of categories. What about Australians? Polynesians? The Ainu of Japan?

Categorizing people is important to any society. It is, at some basic psychological level, probably necessary to have group identity about who and what you are, in contrast to who and what you are not. The concept of race, however, specifically involves the recruitment of biology to validate those categories of self-identity.

Mice don't have to worry about that the way humans do. Consequently, classifying them into subspecies entails less of a responsibility for a scientist than classifying humans into sub-species does. And by the 1960s, most anthropologists realized they could not defend any classification of *Homo sapiens* into biological subspecies or races that could be considered reasonably objective. They therefore stopped doing it, and stopped identifying the endeavor as a central goal of the field. It was a biologically intractable problem—the old square-peg-in-a round-hole enterprise; and people's lives, or welfares, could well depend on the ostensibly scientific pronouncement. Reflecting on the social history of the twentieth century, that was a burden anthropologists would no longer bear.

This conceptual divorce in anthropology—of cultural from biological phenomena was one of the most fundamental scientific revolutions of our time. And since it affected assumptions so rooted in our everyday experience, and resulted in conclusions so counterintuitive—like the idea that the earth goes around the sun, and not vice-versa—it has been widely underappreciated.

Kurt Vonnegut, in *Slaughterhouse Five*, describes what he remembered being taught about human variation: "At that time, they were teaching that there was absolutely no difference between anybody. They may be teaching that still." Of course there are biological differences between people, and between populations. The question is: How are those differences patterned? And the answer seems to be: Not racially. Populations are the only readily identifiable units of humans, and even they are fairly fluid, biologically similar to populations nearby, and biologically different from populations far away.

In other words, the message of contemporary anthropology is: You may group humans into a small number of races if you want to, but you are denied biology as a support for it.

---

New York-born Jonathan Marks earned an undergraduate degree in natural science at Johns Hopkins. After getting his Ph.D. in anthropology, Marks did a post-doc in genetics at the University of California at Davis and is now an associate professor of anthropology at Yale University. He is the coauthor, with Edward Staski, of the introductory textbook *Evolutionary Anthropology* (San Diego: Harcourt, Brace Jovanovich, 1992). His new book, *Human Biodiversity: Genes, Race, and History* is published (1995) by Aldine de Gruyter.

# SECTION II:
*Primatology*

# SECTION II: *Primatology*

# 5 FLO AND HER FAMILY

## Jane Goodall

Old Flo lay on her back in the early morning sunshine her belly full of palm nuts, and suspended Flint above her, grasping one of his minute wrists with her large horny foot. As he dangled, gently saving his free arm and kicking with his legs, she reached up and tickled him in his groin and his neck until he opened his mouth in the place-face, or chimpanzee smile. Nearby Fifi sat staring at Flint, occasionally reaching out to touch her ten-week-old brother gently with one hand.

Faben and Figan, Flo's two elder sons, played with each other not far away. Since Flint's birth two and a half months earlier Faben had begun to move around with his family more frequently. Every so often, as their game became extra vigorous, I could hear the panting chuckles of chimpanzee laughter. All at once Faben, three or four years Figan's senior, began to play rather roughly, sitting down and kicking with the soles of his feet on Figan's bent head. After a few moments Figan had had enough. He left Faben, and, with his jaunty walk, approached Fifi and tried to play with her. At that moment Flo, gathering Flint to her breast, got up to move into the shade, and Fifi pulled away from Figan to follow her mother. Ever since Hugo and I had returned to the Gombe Stream when Flint was seven weeks old, Fifi had become increasingly fascinated by her new brother.

Flo sat down and began to tickle Flint's neck with small nibbling movements of her worn teeth, and Fifi once again sat close and reached out to make a few grooming movements on Flint's back. Flo ignored this. Earlier, though, when Flint was not yet two months old, Flo had usually pushed Fifi's hand away each time she tried to touch Flint, and often the only way in which the child had been able to momentarily touch the infant had been by solicitously grooming Flo, working ever closer and closer to those places where Flint's hands gripped his mother's hair. Intently Fifi had groomed around the hands, occasionally briefly fondling the minute fingers and then, with a glance at Flo, hastily returning to her grooming.

# FLO AND HER FAMILY

Now, however, Flint was older and for the most part Fifi was permitted to touch him. As I watched, Fifi began to play with Flint, taking one hand and nibbling the fingers. Flint gave a soft whimper—possibly Fifi had hurt him— and instantly Flo pushed her daughter's hand away and cuddled her infant close. Frustrated, Fifi rocked slightly to and fro, twisting her arms behind her head and staring at Flint, her lips slightly pouted. It was not long before she reached out, gently this time, to touch him again.

I have always thought that human children become increasingly fascinating as they grow out of the helpless baby stage and begin to respond to people and things. Certainly a chimpanzee baby becomes more attractive as it grows older, not only to its mother and siblings but also to the other members of the community—and to mere human observers. For Hugo and me the privilege of being able to watch Flint's progress that year remains one of the most delightful of our experiences—comparable only to the joy we were to know much later as we watched our own son growing up.

When Flint was three months old he was able to pull himself about on Flo's body, taking handfuls of her hair, pulling with his arms and pushing with his feet. And at this time he began to respond when Fifi approached by reaching out toward her. Fifi became more and more preoccupied with him. She began to make repeated attempts to pull him away from his mother. At first Flo firmly prevented this, but even when Fifi persisted, continually pulling at her brother, Flo never punished her. Sometimes she pushed the child's hand away, sometimes she simply walked away, leaving Fifi rocking slightly, her limbs contorted. And sometimes, when Fifi was extra troublesome, Flo instead of repulsing her advances either groomed her or played with her quite vigorously. These activities usually served to distract Fifi's attention, at least temporarily, from her infant brother.

As the year wore on it seemed that Flo, perhaps as a result of playing so often with her two younger children, became even more playful. Often, as the weeks passed, we saw her playing with both Figan and twelve-year-old Faben, tickling them or chasing with them round and round a tree trunk with Flint hanging on for dear life. On one occasion, in the middle of a romp with Faben, this old female lowered her balding head to the ground, raised her bony rump in the air, and actually turned a

somersault. And then, almost as though she felt slightly ridiculous, she moved away, sat down, and began to groom Flint very carefully.

When Flint was thirteen weeks old we saw Fifi succeed in pulling him away from his mother. Flo was grooming Figan when Fifi, with infinite caution and many quick glances toward her mother's face, began to pull at Flint's foot. Inch by inch she drew the infant toward her—and all at once he was in her arms. Fifi lay on her back and cuddled Flint to her tummy with her arms and legs. She lay very still.

To our surprise Flo for the first few moments appeared to take no notice at all. But when Flint, who had possibly never lost contact with his mother's body, reached around and held his arms toward her, pouting his lips and uttering a soft *hoo* of distress, Flo instantly gathered him to her breast and bent to kiss his head with her lips. Flint eagerly sought the reassurance of his mother's breast, suckling for a few moments before turning to look at Fifi again. And Fifi, her hands clasped behind her head, her elbows in the air, stared at Flint. Ten minutes later Fifi was again permitted to hold Flint for a short while but, once more, the moment Flint gave his tiny distressed whimper Flo rescued him; and Flint, as before, suckled briefly when he regained the security of his mother's arms.

After this not a day passed without Fifi pulling her infant brother away from Flo. As time went on Flint became accustomed to the arms of his sibling, and she was able to hold him for longer periods before he uttered the tiny sound that for the next nine months would bring Flo hastening to his rescue. Flo even permitted Fifi to carry Flint when the family wandered through the forests.

On those occasions when Flo and her family were part of a large group, however, Flo was more possessive of her infant. Then if Fifi moved away with Flint, Flo followed, uttering soft whimpers herself, until she caught up with the kidnaper and retrieved her infant. Even now Fifi was not punished; Flo simply reached forward, grabbed hold of her daughter's ankle, and then gathered Flint into her arms. Sometimes Fifi led her old mother a merry dance, around trees, under low vegetation, where Flo had to creep almost on her belly—even up into the trees. And sometimes, as if to prevent Flo from catching hold of her, she walked backward in front of her mother, grunting softly and bobbing up and down as though in submission, but not—until she was forced to—relinquishing Flint.

When Flint was very small his two elder brothers, although they sometimes stared at him, paid him little attention. Occasionally while he was grooming with his mother, Faben very gently patted the infant; Figan, though he was such an integral part of the family, seemed afraid to touch Flint in the early days. If, when Figan and Flo were grooming, the infant accidentally touched Figan, as in baby fashion he waved his arms about, Figan, after a quick glance at Flo's face, seemed to avoid looking at Flint. For Figan, though he was a vigorous adolescent male, still showed great respect for his old mother.

One occasion is vivid in my memory. Fifi had taken Flint and was sitting grooming the infant some ten yards from Flo. When Figan approached and sat beside his sister, Flint turned toward him and, with his wide-eyed gaze fixed on Figan's face, reached out to grasp his brother's chest hair. Figan started, and after a quick glance in Flo's direction raised his hands up and away from the infant. Then he stayed motionless, staring down at Flint, his lips tense. The infant pulled closer and nuzzled at Figan's breast, then all at once seemed afraid of the unfamiliar. Usually his only contacts were Flo and Fifi, and if he reached toward either of them they always responded by holding him close. With a slight pout Flint turned back to Fifi, but then, as though confused, he again reached to Figan with a soft whimper. At this Flo came hurrying to his rescue, and as she approached Figan too gave low worried cries, and raised his hands even higher as in the age-old gesture of surrender. Flo gathered up her infant and Figan lowered his hands slowly, as though dazed.

One day, when Flint was just less than five months old, Flo got up to go and, instead of pressing Flint to her belly, took his arm in one hand and hoisted him over her shoulder onto her back. There he remained for a few yards before he slipped down and clung to her arm. For a short distance Flo continued, with Flint gripping around her elbow; then she pushed him back under her tummy. The next day when Flo arrived in camp, Flint was clinging precariously to her back, hanging on to her sparse hair with his hands and feet. When Flo left she again pushed her son up onto her back, and again he clung there awhile before sliding down and dangling from one hand by her side. This time, after walking thirty yards or so, Flo pushed him once more onto

her back. After this Flint nearly always rode on Flo's back or else dangled beside her while she walked the mountains. This was not surprising, since all infants after a certain age start riding their mothers rather than clinging on beneath; but we were astonished to see that Fifi, when next we saw her take Flint, also tried to push him onto her back. This was surely an example of learning by direct observation of her mother's behavior.

By the time Flint was five months old he had become an accomplished rider, and only occasionally slipped down to dangle beside Flo as she walked. If there was any sign of excitement among the group, or if Flo was about to move into thick undergrowth, then she always reached back and pushed Flint around so that he clung underneath as before. Soon he learned to wriggle under Flo of his own accord in response to the slightest touch.

About the same time Flint began to ride on Flo's back we first saw him take a step by himself. For some weeks previously he had been able to stand on the ground balanced on three limbs and clinging to Flo's hair with one hand; and occasionally he had taken a couple of steps in this manner. On this particular morning he suddenly let go of Flo and stood by himself, all four limbs on the ground. Then, very deliberately, he lifted one hand off the ground, moved it forward safely, and paused. He lifted a foot off the ground, lurched sideways, staggered, and fell on his nose with a whimper. Instantly Flo reached out and scooped him into her arms. But that was the beginning. Each day after this Flint walked one or two steps farther, although for months he was incredibly wobbly. Constantly he got his hands and feet muddled up and fell—and always Flo was quick to gather him up. Often she kept one hand under his tummy as he tottered along.

Just after he began to walk Flint attempted to climb. One day we saw him standing upright, holding on to a tiny sapling with both hands and gripping it first with one foot and then the other. But he never managed to get both feet off the ground at once and after a few moments he fell backward onto the ground. Subsequently he repeated this performance several times and Flo, as she groomed Fifi, idly held one hand behind his back, preventing further tumbles. A week after his first attempt Flint was able to climb a short way quite easily. Like a human child, he found it much harder to get down by himself. Flo of course was very watchful—as indeed was Fifi—and one or other of his guardians reached to rescue him the moment he gave his soft whimper. Flo, in fact, often retrieved him when she noticed that the end of the branch on which he was swinging was beginning to bend and Flint was totally unaware of it. She was equally quick to seize him if she saw any sign of social excitement or aggression among other members of the group.

Gradually Flint learned to control his limbs slightly better when walking, although he still often relied on speed, rather than coordination, to get him from one place to another. He began to venture several yards away from Flo—and since any movement away from his mother was wildly exciting, and excitement set his hair on end, he tottered around like a fluffy black ball, his wide-eyed gaze fixed with concentration on some object or individual in front of him.

It was at this time that fascination for her small brother became almost an obsession of Fifi's. She spent nearly all her day laying with him, grooming him as he slept, or carrying him about with her. Flo, it seemed, was often far from displeased to shed from time to time part of her load of maternal responsibility. Provided that Fifi did not carry Flint out of sight, and provided there were no potentially aggressive males nearby, she no longer objected when Fifi kidnapped Flint. Nor did Flo seem to mind if other youngsters approached Flint to play gently with him. But Fifi did. If she suddenly noticed Gilka, or another of her erstwhile playmates, close to Flint, Fifi instantly abandoned whatever she was doing, rushed over and chased the youngster away, hair bristling, arms flailing, and feet stamping the ground. Even chimps much older than herself, provided they were subordinate to Flo, were threatened or even attacked by aggressive Fifi. Presumably she acted on the assumption that if anything went wrong old Flo would hurry to her assistance—and it was more evident that the victims of her fury were fully aware of this fact also.

Fifi, however, could not chase Faben or Figan away from Flint, and as the infant grew up both of this elder brothers showed the increasing interest in him. Often they would approach and play with him, tickling him or pushing him gently to and fro as he dangled, legs kicking, from a low branch. Sometimes when Figan was playing with Flint, we saw Fifi hurry to the scene and try to initiate a game with Figan; many times she was successful. Then, when the game was over, Fifi would hurry back to play with Flint herself. Was she, perhaps, practicing the same technique of distraction that Flo had used so often on her?

When Flint tottered up to one of the adult males, Fifi could scarcely interfere; she merely sat and stared as David, or Goliath, or Mike reached out and time and again patted Flint or gently embraced him. And as the weeks went by Flint, like a spoiled human child, wanted more and more attention. One day as he tottered up to Mr. McGregor the old male got up and moved away. It was not, I think, deliberate—it just happened that he was about to leave. Flint stopped dead, staring with widening eyes at the male's retreating rear, and then, stumbling along with frantic haste, repeatedly falling on his face, Flint followed. Continuously he uttered his soft whimper. Within moments Flo was rushing to retrieve him. That was only the start of it, and for the next few weeks Flint was always whimpering along after one or other of the adult males who had not deigned to stop and greet him, or who had walked away from the infant for any reason whatever. Often the male concerned, uneasy perhaps at the little calls following in his wake, would stop or turn back to pat Flint.

When Flint was eight months old he sometimes spent fifteen minutes or so out of contact with Flo as he played or explored, but he was never far from her. He was somewhat steadier on his feet and he was able to join Fifi in some of her slightly rougher games, chasing around a grass tuft, or pulling himself on top of her as she lay on the ground and tickling her with his hands and mouth. It was at this time that the termiting season began.

One day when Flo was fishing for termites it became obvious that Figan and Fifi, who had been eating termites at the same heap, were becoming restless and wanted to leave. Old Flo, who had already fished for two hours and was herself only getting about two termites every five minutes, showed no signs of stopping. Being an old female, it was possible that she might continue for another hour at least. Several times Figan had set off resolutely along the track leading to the stream, but on each occasion, after repeatedly looking back at Flo, he had given up and returned to wait for his mother.

Flint, too young to mind where he was, pottered about on the heap, occasionally dabbing at a termite. Suddenly

Figan got up and again this time approached Flint. Adopting the posture of a mother who signals her infant to climb onto her back, Figan bent one leg and reached back his hand to Flint, uttering a soft, pleading wimper. Flint tottered up to him at once, and Figan, still whimpering, put his hand under Flint and gently pushed him onto his back. Once Flint was safely aboard, Figan, with another quick glance at Flo, set off rapidly along the track. A moment later Flo discarded her tool and followed.

Hugo and I were amazed at this further example of Figan's ingenuity in getting his own way. Had his behavior really been deliberate? We couldn't be sure. A few days later Fifi did exactly the same thing. A week later we watched Faben take Flint to his breast after he too had tried several times to persuade his mother to follow him away from a termite heap. We had never seen Faben carrying Flint before.

As the termite season wore on there could be no doubt that Flo's older offspring were kidnaping Flint with the deliberate intent of getting their mother to stop, at least for the time being, her endless termiting. We saw all three of them taking Flint in this way on any number of occasions. They were not always successful. Often Flint dropped off and ran back to his mother of his own accord. And sometimes, if Flo's hole was still yielding a good supply of termites, she hurried to retrieve Flint and then returned to the heap followed by the unsuccessful kidnapper—who usually tried again later.

Flint, of course, was too young to show any interest in eating termites; he occasionally sampled a mouthful of fig or banana but still received virtually all his nourishment from his mother's milk, and would continue to do so for another year. Once in a while he did poke at a crawling termite with his finger, and he played with discarded grass tools when he was wandering about on a termite heap. Also, he began to "mop" everything. When termites are spilled onto the surface of the heap, older chimps mop them up with the backs of their wrists: the termites become entangled in the hairs and are picked off with the lips. It was soon after the termite season began that Flint started to mop things—the ground, his own legs, his mother's back as he rode along, anything but termites. Actually, though he sometimes gazed intently for a few moments as his mother or one of his siblings worked, he was not really interested in this activity which so absorbed his elders.

Fifi, on the other hand, was a keen termite fisher, and when Flint, wanting to play with his sister, jumped onto her and scattered the insects from her grass stem, she was obviously irritated. Over and over she pushed him away roughly. Fifi still played with Flint frequently herself when she was not termiting, but, almost as though some spell had been broken, she never again showed quite the same fanatical preoccupation with him; she no longer protected him as consistently from social contact with other young chimps.

Flint then began to enlarge his circle of friends, since Fifi, particularly when she was working at a termite heap, often permitted Gilka or one of the other juveniles to approach and play with Flint. She no longer rushed up aggressively every time one or other of the adolescent females carried Flint around or groomed him or played with him. Flint, in fact, was growing up.

Even when Fifi did devote all her attention to her little brother she could no longer treat him as her doll, for he had developed a mind of his own. If Fifi wanted to carry him in one direction and he wanted to go somewhere else, then he struggled away from her and went his way. Also, he was getting heavier. One day when Flint was sleeping in her lap and gripping tightly to her hair, it was obvious that he was hurting his sister. Fifi carefully detached first one hand and then the other, but as soon as they were loosened Flint, disturbed, gripped on again tightly. Finally, for the first time on record Fifi carried the infant back to Flo and pushed him in her mother's direction.

When Flint was one year old he was still wobbly on his legs but he was quick to bounce toward any game in progress, and eager to hurry over to greet any newcomer that joined his group. He was, in fact, beginning to take part in the social life of his community: a community which at that time was still unsettled as a result of the dramatic rise to overall dominance of Mike. Flint could scarcely have been aware of the battle of wills that had finally led to Goliath's defeat because it had started at the time of his birth. Flint grew up in a world where Mike undisputedly was supreme.

# 6 KARISOKE FIELD IMPRESSIONS

Dian Fossey

My knowledge of Kabara's fate, as gained from the air, made the research at Karisoke seem more imperative than ever. However, even the prospect of unknown gorillas to identify and habituate did not ease my mind about the destiny of the Kabara population. At Kabara I had studied three groups totaling 50 individuals. During the first year at Karisoke I concentrated observations on four main groups that totaled 51 individuals living within the 9 1/2 square-mile study area around camp. These groups, identified by number according to the order in which contacted, were Groups 4, 5, 8, and 9. Other groups encountered were considered fringe groups whose ranges either abutted or overlapped those of the main study groups, or were totally unhabituated groups met during census work on other mountains.

Since I tried to distribute observation hours evenly among the four main study groups, lapses of several days could occur between successive contacts with any one of them. My tracking ability of necessity improved, because the trails were older and longer than if each group had been tracked daily, and the Rwandese on my staff were yet to become skilled trackers.

A good six months were to pass before the men felt confident enough to go out into the forest and track by themselves. Even then, they clearly preferred not going more than an hour from camp and were reluctant to follow trails older than two or three days because of the distances involved. With old trails two trackers, rather than one, went out together. Much of the terrain was still unfamiliar to them and they retained a natural apprehension of possible encounters with wildlife or poachers.

Teaching Rwandese how to track was far easier than instructing the students who eventually came to Karisoke. The locals' senses, especially their eyesight, were more acute. When training anyone, I always led the way for a couple of days, explaining the factors that determined the route taken. Sometimes I purposely strayed from an actual gorilla trail (occasionally unintentionally) to see how long it would take those behind me to realize the error. Another beneficial teaching ruse was furtively to press a series of my own knuckleprints along a section of damp earth going in the opposite direction to the knuckleprints of the gorillas being followed. How Sanwekwe would have loved this bit of chicanery! Those being trained would excitedly discover my knuckleprints and confidently follow them only to find no gorilla spoor ahead. This method proved to be the best way to teach people not to blunder about when on difficult trails—trails on grassy meadows or rocky slopes in particular, where even one bootprint can destroy a vital tracking clue.

Following gorilla track in thick herbaceous foliage is in fact child's play. Most vegetation bends in the direction of a group's travel, knuckleprints may be found impressed upon intermittent dirt patches or trails, and chains of gorilla dung deposits provide other clues as to the direction of the animals' passage. The individuals of a calmly moving group do not travel one after another. There may be nearly as many trails as group members, so I attempt always to follow the most central trail. Numerous cul-de-sacs occur wherever individuals depart from the main route to go off and feed by themselves. I learned eventually that the false leads could be identified by the presence of two layers of foliage. The top one is bent in the direction of the group's travel and the lower is bent in the opposite direction where an individual has gone off on its own before returning to follow the group.

In extremely dense, tall foliage, much circuitous tracking time could be saved by looking ahead of a group's trail for signs of disturbance of vegetation or of branches in distant trees where gorillas have climbed to feed. This technique was especially helpful in the saddle areas, where gorilla spoor could be nearly eradicated by passage of elephant or large herds of buffalo. The ground signs that might survive between the miniature craters left by the elephants' feet are the gorillas' typical trilocular dung deposits or their feeding remnants, such as the unmistakable peelings of thistle and celery stalks. Often, gorilla trail merges briefly with or zigzags in and out of buffalo trail. Whenever this happens and visual clues are obscured by vegetation I feel with my fingertips for the deep imprints left by the cloven hooves of the buffalo to realize that I am on the wrong path. Because gorillas always seek fresh untrampled vegetation for feeding purposes, they seldom travel along buffalo trails for any distance.

Unfortunately, the reverse is not true. Characteristically bovine in nature, buffalo are very trail-oriented, particularly in thick vegetation. Upon encountering gorilla trails, they often follow them like so many cows heading for the barn. On several occasions, without intention I found myself following gorillas who were in turn being followed by buffalo. Twice the gorillas, either in vexation or perhaps with a sense of joie-de-vivre, turned and charged directly toward the buffalo, which speedily turned tail and retreated unknowingly toward me. In retrospect, the subsequent confrontations had all the comical ingredients of a Laurel and Hardy movie. I had the option of climbing any available tree or diving headfirst into vegetation — too often nettles—that fringed the trail of the oncoming herd. I was always more than willing to let buffalo have the right-of-way. This is one of the first rules any person must learn when working in the domain of wild animals and is one that some learn the hard way.

Tracking is an enjoyable challenge, though there were times when trackers became convinced that their four-legged quarry had sprouted wings, so faint were the clues. This was especially true when trying to follow the trail of a lone silverback gorilla rather than a group, trails more than a week old, crossing relatively barren regions as meadows or lava rockslides, and traversed by ungulates sharing gorillas' terrain.

One morning along the trail of a lone silverback I was belly-crawling under a long dank tunnel roofed by a fallen *Hagenia* tree and sided by dense vines. With relief I saw a sunlit opening about fifteen feet ahead and wormed toward it enthusiastically while dragging my knapsack behind me. Upon reaching it I grabbed on to what appeared to be the base of a sapling in order to pull myself out of the gloomy tunnel confines. The intended support not only hauled me out of the tunnel but dragged me through several feet of nettles before I had the sense to let go of the left leg of a very surprised buffalo. The odoriferous deposits of his justifiable fright took several days to wash out of my hair and clothing. Much can be gained by crawling, rather than walking, along gorilla trail, a fact I discovered one day by accident. Traces of a silverback's pungent body odor, resembling human nondeodorized sweat smell, permeated vegetation the gorilla had traveled through some twenty-four hours previously. Had I been walking after the lone silverback that day rather than crawling, I never would have realized the importance of olfactory clues existing at ground level. There are two types of sweat glands existing in gorilla skin. The axillary region of the adult male contains four to seven layers of large apocrine glands responsible for the powerful fear odor of the silverback, an odor only weakly transmitted by the adult female. The palms and soles of males and females contain apocrine glands and a high concentration of eccrine glands that have an important lubrication function. Both types of gland would appear to be evolutionary adaptations for terrestrial travel and olfactory communication, particularly for adult male gorillas.

The most outstanding odor found along fresh gorilla trail emanates from the dung deposits. Healthy gorillas leave chains of dung lobes similar in texture and smell to those of horses. When gorillas travel at an unhurried pace, the three-lobed sections may be deposited in a chain with the lobes attached to one another by strands of fibrous vegetation. If the animals have been feeding on fruit such as wild blackberries (*Rubus runssorensis*) or the plum-sized *Pygeum africanum*, the seeds, or even the whole fruit, can be found intact in the dung and can provide clues as to where the group had been ranging. The relative age of dung can be determined by the number of flies swarming around it, as well as the amount of eggs the flies have laid on the dung's surface. Countless hundreds of small white eggs are laid within minutes following defecation and begin hatching within eight to twelve hours, the variation dependent on the weather. Weather always has to be considered when determining the age of a trail. Sunny warm days make fresh spoor, such as dung or foliage discards, appear old by drying them out after only a few hours of exposure, whereas rain or heavy mist have exactly the opposite effect. I found it helpful during the early days of the study to return to camp with fresh dung specimens and vegetation discards and then record their aging process under various weather conditions. Repetition of this simple procedure soon improved my ability to gauge the age of trails accurately. To evaluate distances more precisely I set up stakes outside the tent, 50 to 250 feet apart, so that actual rather than approximate measures became familiar.

The dung of lactating females is often covered with a whitish sheath, possibly a result of the tendency gorilla mothers have to eat the feces of their offspring during the infant's first four to six months of life. Diarrhetic dung, either with or without a mucoid sheath or flecks of blood, when deposited by only one individual of a group,

often signifies that the individual is ill. When numerous animals of a group leave diarrhetic dung along a trail, it is an indication that the gorillas have been alarmed by another group or, more likely, by poachers. These types of deposits are always found on flee trails created when a group has rapidly run, almost single file, from a potential threat. The time I spend following a flee trail seems horridly prolonged because of growing apprehensions about what may be found at the end of it.

Occasionally, various groups acquire a communal cestode parasite (*Anoplocephala gorillae*), an infection that could not be correlated with either seasonal or range patterns. Large flatworm segments, about 1 inch long, are most frequently found in feces deposited in night nests and, when examined early in the morning, the dung contents of the nests seem virtually alive, crawling with activity.

All age and sex classes of gorillas have been observed eating their own dung and, to a lesser extent, that of other gorillas. Coprophagy is most likely to occur after prolonged day-resting periods during the rainy season, when both feeding and travel time are minimized. The animals simply shift their buttocks slightly to catch the dung lobe in one hand before it contacts the earth. They then bite into the lobe and while chewing smack their lips with apparent relish. The eating of excrement occurs among most vertebrates, including humans, who have certain nutritional deficiencies. Among gorillas coprophagy is thought to have possible dietary functions because it may allow vitamins, particularly Vitamin $B_{12}$ synthesized in the hind gut, to be assimilated in the foregut. Since the activity is usually observed during periods of cold wet weather, I am inclined to relate the "meals" to instant warmed TV dinners!

Between age and sex classes dung sizes vary tremendously, ranging from around 3 inches for silverbacks, to 3/8-1 inch for infants. Analyzing the dung contents of the night nests makes it possible to determine the composition of fringe or census groups, and is also a reliable means of learning if births or transfers have occurred within study groups. (Most births occur during the night and night nests contain nearly half of the dung deposited by an individual over a twenty-four-hour period.)

Gorillas are diurnal and build their nests in different locations each evening. Ninety-eight percent of gorillas' night nests are built from nonfood vegetation, since food items such as thistles, nettles, and celery are not suitable nesting material. Adult night nests are sturdy, compact structures, sometimes resembling oval, leafy bathtubs made from bulky plants such as Lobelia (*Lobelia giberroa*) and Senecio (*Senecioerici-rosenii*). Construction is concentrated on the rim of the nest, which is composed of multiple bent stalks, the leafy ends of which are tucked around and under the animal's body for a more "cushiony" central bottom. Nests can be built in trees as well as on the ground, but because of adult gorillas' great weight nests are more commonly found on the ground. Favored nesting locations during the rainy season are in the sheltered hollows of tree trunks and nests may be made only of moss or loose soil. These types of nests not only offer protection from the elements but also provide early morning snacks in the form of decayed tree bark and roots.

Nests built by immatures are often only flimsy clusters of leaves until practice enables the construction of a solid, serviceable nest. The youngest animal observed consistently building and sleeping within his own night nest was thirty-four months old. Ordinarily a youngster remains sleeping in the mother's nest until the female again gives birth.

Some degree of predetermination is shown in the choice of night-nesting sites when gorillas are in areas adjacent to the park boundaries or near routes frequently used by poachers. The animals then tend to select knolls or open slopes offering good vantage points from which to view the surrounding terrain. This same type of choice also occurs when other gorilla groups are nearby. Less selectivity is demonstrated in the choice of day-nesting sites, although on sunny days areas with optimal sun exposure are far more frequently used than shaded or heavily treed regions.

For many years the slopes immediately behind camp were a part of the ranges of Groups 4 and 5. On dozens of occasions I found that the females and younger group members built their night nests about one hundred feet up on the slope near camp, whereas the silverbacks nested at the hill's base. This arrangement made it almost impossible for anyone to approach the gorillas undetected. When either Group 4 or 5 nested behind camp, I would approach them cautiously the following dawn in the hope of observing the animals before they awoke. Without fail I would almost step on a sleeping silverback sentry obscured

in the tall foliage at the base of the slope. It was difficult to know which of us was the more shocked as the rudely awakened animal instantly jumped to his feet screaming in alarm before, running uphill to "defend" his family, all now thoroughly awakened.

Vestiges of tree nests last as long as four years, far longer than those constructed in ground foliage, which last some five months, depending upon weather conditions or location. Clusters of night nests made from tall lobelia plants often yield interesting information concerning the frequency and length of gorillas' use of certain areas. Lobelias continue to grow in height even after their top leafy crowns have been broken off for nests. I have estimated that these plants grow about two or three inches a year. An area containing circles of lobelia stalks, some 10 feet tall, suggests that nesting sites were perhaps built there about thirty years earlier.

There is some speculation that night nests either offer protection from the weather or may be an innate activity remaining from gorillas ancestral tree living prototypes. Both points of view are plausible. I have observed numerous zoo gorillas born in captivity who apparently innately, rather than imitatively, utilized any remotely suitable object to shape around or under their bodies, much in the same manner that free-living gorillas use vegetation. Once I watched a lady's large straw hat blow into a zoo enclosure and be immediately retrieved by an adult female gorilla. The animal painstakingly ripped the hat into shreds to "build" a flimsy nest around herself while staunchly defending her nesting material against the other individuals in the cage.

Normally gorilla groups spend about 40 percent of their days resting, 30 percent feeding, and 30 percent traveling or travel-feeding—times when both movement and eating occur simultaneously. Around the Karisoke Research Centre's study area of 9 1/2 square miles there are seven major vegetation zones, each attractive to gorillas at various times of the year according to weather and season.

The saddle zone is relatively flat terrain lying between the three westerly volcanoes (Mts. Visoke, Karisimbi, and Mikeno) and interspersed with hills and ridges no more than 98 feet high. The saddle contains the richest variety of vines and herbaceous ground foliage, in addition to having the highest frequency of *Hagenia* and *Hypericum* trees.

The *Vernonia* zone is found in small areas of the saddle as well as on the lower slopes of Visoke. The flowers, bark, and pulp of *Vernonia* trees are favored gorilla food. This tree species is so frequently selected for nesting and play activities that it is becoming increasingly rare in some areas of previous abundance.

The nettle zone is found in small sections of the saddle and on the lower Visoke slopes, but the main nettle area lies at the western base of Visoke in a dense belt varying in width from one to two fifths of a mile.

The bamboo zone is a limited region found primarily along the eastern boundary of the park and is responsible for seasonal movements of Group 5. Only a few isolated clumps of bamboo grow in the saddle of Group 4's range, but when the bamboo begins shooting, the group leaves the mountain slopes and unerringly travels straight to the bamboo clumps, indicating their keen recollection of both season and location of food sources.

The brush zone is found mainly along ridges of Visoke's slopes and, to a lesser extent, on hills in the saddle. I consider it a separate zone because it contains a high density of favored fruit shrubs and trees, such as blackberry and *Pygeum*, and rarer trees and brush whose bark is avidly sought by the gorillas.

The giant lobelia zone is found 11,480 to 12,465 feet on Visoke's upper slopes. This area is frequented by gorillas during drier months when the high mountain vegetation retains moisture from nightly mists. For this reason succulence can be obtained from the brush, trees, and foliage characteristic of the region.

The Afro-alpine zone encompasses the highest portion of the mountain summits and consists mainly of open grass or lichen-covered meadows. This is a sparse, bleak area containing little gorilla vegetation.

Gorillas travel more rapidly in areas where food resources are limited, and also when they are undertaking "exploratory sallies"—treks into unfamiliar terrain. Such ventures appear to be the means by which either a lone silverback or a group can expand its saddlezone range. Range expansion into the saddle avoids extensive overlapping with other groups, as was the case on Visoke's slopes in the late 1960s. Often when tracking gorillas on these long crosscountry treks, I whimsically pictured the silverbacks urging on their group members by saying, "Okay guys, let's just see what's on the other side of this next little hill!" Frequently the animals ended up in totally unsuitable gorilla habitat and had to traverse back and forth in order to find small oases containing food vegetation before renewing their quest for satisfactory terrain. Sometimes their travel routes were so erratic that I became certain, especially on foggy days when the mountaintops were hidden from view, that the animals were either lost or extremely disoriented.

Acquisition of new range area is more often achieved within the saddle zone than on the slopes, because the saddle's expansive land surface offers a greater abundance and variety of preferred vegetation. Gorillas feed upon some fifty-eight plant species from the seven zones in the study area. Leaves, shoots, and stems form about 86 percent of the diet and fruits only 2 percent. Dung, dirt, bark, roots, grubs, and snails are also eaten, but to a far lesser extent than foliage. The most common herbaceous plants consumed are thistles, nettles, and celery—which could grow up to eight feet. The scraggly *Galium* vine forms the bulk of the gorillas' diet, most likely because it, unlike other vegetation, grows at nearly all levels of the forest from amid thick ground foliage to the tops of tree branches, where it is more easily obtained by agile immatures than by adults.

There is the possibility that gorillas improve their habitat within tall herbaceous vegetation both in the saddle and on the mountain slopes. Cattle and buffalo, with their corneous, sharp hooves, sever plant stems underfoot; but gorillas' hands and feet, with their padded soles, press herbaceous foliage into the earth, and thereby cause more rapid regeneration because of the increased number of shoots sprouting from the nodes of the semiburied stems. By marking off small plots of foliage traversed only by gorillas, some plots frequented only by bovines, and the remaining used by neither, I was able to see, within a six-week period, that the sections covered by gorillas had a far denser growth of vegetation, particularly nettles and thistles.

Competition over food resources is seldom observed among gorillas unless the sources of favored food are restricted by short seasonal growth or clumped in small areas. One such example is the *Pygeum* fruit tree that grows oaklike about 60 feet tall and is found only on a few mountain ridges. Because of the relative scarcity of the trees and their brief fruiting season—only two to three months a year—the ridges that support them attract concentrations of gorilla groups all at one time. It is a spectacular sight to watch massive silverbacks gingerly climbing to the highest branches in search of the small delicacies. Because of status, silverbacks have first culling choice while animals of lesser rank wait their turns at the bottom until the patriarchs descend. After gathering mouthfuls and handfuls of the fruit, the gorillas skillfully maneuver themselves to the nearest sturdy perch upon which to sit and enjoy their meager harvest.

Another scarce and keenly sought food is related to mistletoe. At altitudes around 10,000 feet it grows on spindly trees such as *Hypericum*. Thus immature animals are able to collect the leafy flowered stalks more proficiently than weighty adults who frequently have to sit under trees waiting for *Loranthus* tidbits to fall their way. Youngsters who make the mistake of painstakingly descending to the forest floor to eat their collection more comfortably are usually bothered by pilfering adults who have no trouble "bullying" the young out of their acquisitions.

Still another special food is bracket fungus (*Ganoderma applanatum*), a parasitical tree growth resembling a large solidified mushroom. The shelflike projection is difficult to break free from a tree, so younger animals often have to wrap their arms and legs awkwardly around a trunk and content themselves by only gnawing at the delicacy. Older animals who succeed in breaking the fungus loose have been observed carrying it several hundred feet from its source, all the while guarding it possessively from more dominant individuals' attempts to take it away. Both the scarcity of the fungus and the gorillas' liking of it cause many intragroup squabbles, a number of which are settled by the silverback, who simply takes the item of contention for himself.

Group disputes also arise when restricted feeding sites containing prized foods create crowded conditions. The most common example occurs whenever an entire group seeks access to limited bamboo patches such as are found in the saddle zone. This also happens in the dry months when gorillas go on soil-eating binges on Visoke's ridges, where some earth is particularly rich in calcium and potassium. For many years one cavernous "dig" was favored by Group 5. The ridge supporting numerous trees had been so dug out by the gorillas that the tree roots formed exposed gnarled supports for the vast caves created by the animals' repeated soil digging.

Upon approaching this region, the leader of Group 5 went first as a matter of course, while other group members resigned themselves to waiting outside the favored cave. It was eerie to watch the huge silverback magically disappear beneath a web of tree roots into total blackness. When he emerged, covered with the sandy crumbs of his feast, he moved off, leaving the cavern to the other group members. In order of rank, they disappeared into its depths. Their subsequent screams and pig-grunts reflected the overcrowded conditions.

Group 4 chose their dirt mainly from sandy slides. Year after year the slides also attracted swallows to bathe and nest in the loose dirt. Much like Group 5, Group 4 headed for these barren areas during dry seasons to scoop up the soil with their hands and ingest handfuls of dirt. Even after hours of observation at these spots, I never saw gorillas attempt to catch adult swallows, their young, or their eggs.

Since gorillas mainly eat vegetation, food preparation involves manual and oral dexterity, attributes with which gorillas are well endowed. Perhaps for this reason gorillas have not yet been observed fashioning objects within their environment as tools. By contrast, free-living chimpanzees are renowned for their clever adaptations of twigs and leaves to serve as tools for obtaining both food and water.

Possibly gorillas have never been observed improvising tools to obtain food because the resources of their habitat meet their needs. Once, following a four-month dry spell in 1969, swarms of termites passed through the study area. I expected that the gorillas would, chimpanzee style, improvise twigs to extract the termites from the decayed tree stumps. However, they totally ignored the termites and waded their way past the infested areas to feed on surrounding vegetation.

On warm sunny days when group contentment is at its highest, feeding and resting periods are frequently accompanied by soft purring sounds resembling stomach rumbling; thus I named them "belch vocalizations." Typically, one animal expresses its feeling of well-being by giving a series of disyllabic belch vocalizations, naoom, naoom, naoom. This brings a chain of similar responses from other animals nearby, thus establishing both the location and the identification of the individuals participating in the exchange. The sound serves as the perfect communication for humans to imitate when initiating contacts with gorilla groups either partially or totally obscured in vegetation. By its use I can inform the animals of my presence and allay any apprehensions they might have on hearing the noise of vegetation being broken near them. It is an extraordinary feeling to be able to sit in the middle of a resting group of gorillas and contribute to a contented chorus of belch vocalizers. The belch vocalization is the most common form of intragroup communication. In its prolonged form it expresses contentment, though a slightly shortened version may serve as a mild disciplinary rebuke toward young animals. A stronger disciplinary vocalization is the "pig-grunt," a series of harsh, staccato grunts resembling the sounds of pigs feeding at a sty, and frequently used by silverbacks when settling squabbles among other members of their groups. Females direct the vocalization toward other adults when conflicts over food arise or when right-of-way on trails occurs, and also toward their infants, particularly during the last stages of the weaning process. Young individuals will pig-grunt among themselves when complaining during rough play with their siblings or peers.

Popular literature generally describes roars, screams, or wraaghs as the main components of the gorilla vocabulary. Indeed, during the initial part of my study, these were the most frequent sounds I heard from the as yet unhabituated gorillas whenever my presence posed an element of threat to them. Gorilla vocalizations have always interested me, and I have spent many months recording sounds in the field and later analyzing them spectrographically at Cambridge University. The work proved most rewarding when the high frequency of alarm calls was slowly replaced by undisturbed intragroup vocalizations, sounds I used to gain further acceptance by the gorillas.

In late 1972, when student observers began working at Karisoke, instruction in the art of belch vocalizing was one of the first lessons taught. Several newcomers never quite got on to imitating the sound properly. One person's rendition of the belch vocalization sounded exactly like a goat's bleat, but within several weeks, the gorillas even became accustomed to his individual greeting call.

At times, students as well as I have unexpectedly encountered gorillas before we were aware of the animals' nearness. Such occasions could provoke charges, especially if interactions were occurring between groups, when the animals were traveling in a precarious range area (like

one frequented by poachers), or if an infant had recently been born.

Understandably, such circumstances compelled highly protective strategies from a group's silverback leader. Once I was charged when climbing through tall vegetation up a steep hill to meet Group 8, thought to be several hours away. Suddenly, like a pane of broken glass, the air around me was shattered by the screams of the five males of the group as they bulldozed their way down through the foliage toward me. It is very difficult to describe the charge of a gorilla group. As in the other charges I have experienced, the intensity of the gorillas' screams was so deafening, I could not locate the source of the noise. I only knew that the group was charging from above, when the tall vegetation gave way as though an out-of-control tractor were headed directly for me.

Upon recognizing me, the group's dominant silverback swiftly braked to a stop three feet away, causing the four males behind him, momentarily and ungracefully, to pile up on top of him. At this instant I slowly sank to the ground to assume as submissive a pose as possible. The hair on each male's headcrest stood erect (piloerection), canines were fully exposed, the irises of ordinarily soft brown eyes glinted yellow—more like those of cats than of gorillas—and an overpowering fear odor permeated the air. For a good half-hour all five males screamed if I made even the slightest movement. After a thirty-minute period, the group allowed me to pretend to feed meekly on vegetation before they finally moved rigidly out of sight uphill.

Only then could I stand up to check out the cause of human shouting that I had heard coming from the base of the slope about four hundred feet below. There, standing along a trail used extensively for cattle at this early stage of my work, stood a group of Watutsi herdsmen. They had been drawn by the gorillas' screams from various parts of the adjacent forest where they were grazing cattle. I later learned the men were certain I had been torn to shreds, and upon seeing me stand upright were convinced that I was protected by a very special kind of *sumu* against the wrath of the gorillas, whom they feared deeply.

Once the men moved out of sight I continued to follow Group 8—at a distance—to discover that they had been interacting with Group 9 when I had attempted to contact them. Trail sign indicated Group 9 had also taken part in the charge but had halted before reaching me. It was only when descending the slope that I discovered a lone silverback directly below me. His presence made Group 8's charge far more understandable. Upon hearing the sounds of my approach through the thick vegetation, the gorillas probably thought I was the lone male whose presence neither group would have tolerated.

Though you know the charging gorillas are simply acting defensively and do not wish to inflict physical harm, you instinctively want to flee, an impulse that automatically invites a chase. I have always been convinced of the intrinsically gentle nature of gorillas and felt their charges were basically bluff in nature, so never hesitated to hold my ground. However, because of the intensity of their screams and the speed of their approaches, I found it possible to face charging gorillas only by clinging to surrounding vegetation for dear life. Without that support, I surely would have turned tail and run.

Like all charges, this one was really my fault for having climbed the steep slope to approach directly beneath the animals without first identifying myself. Other charges have occurred when students, also accidentally, made the same error. Some census workers who encountered unfamiliar gorilla groups outside the study area had to return to their camps several times to change clothes because of reflexive reactions prompted by charges. People who hold their ground usually are not hurt unless they are unknown to the gorillas, but even then they only occasionally receive a moderate slap from a passing animal. People who run are not so fortunate.

A very capable student once made the same mistake as I had when approaching Group 8 from directly below. He was climbing through extremely dense foliage in a poacher area and noisily hacking at vegetation with his *panga*, not knowing the group was near. The faulty approach provoked a charge from the dominant silverback, who could not see who was coming. When the young man instinctively turned and ran, the male lunged toward the fleeing form. The gorilla knocked him down, tore into his knapsack, and was just beginning to sink his teeth into the student's arm when he recognized a familiar observer. The silverback immediately backed off, wearing what I was told was an "apologetic facial expression" before scurrying back to the rest of Group 8 without even a backward glance.

Another person who ran away from the charge of an unfamiliar group was someone who had always scoffed at the idea of pacifying gorillas with introductory vocalizations on approaching them. His actions around gorillas were often jerky and almost aggressive in nature. He was able to spend nearly a year working with habituated animals before his luck ran out. In the lead of a large boisterous group of tourists he approached two interacting groups from directly below and was instantly charged by a silverback, who rolled with him for some thirty feet, breaking three of his ribs, and then bit deeply into the dorsal surface of the man's neck. The bite would have been fatal had it pierced the jugular vein on the neck's ventral surface. This person survived to brag about his "close shave" without acknowledging his violation of basic gorilla protocol.

In another incident a young tourist tried to pick up an infant from Group 5 "to cuddle" in spite of the alarmed screams given by the group. Before he got his hands on the youngster, the infant's mother and the group's silverback defensively charged, causing the boy to turn and run. He fell and both gorilla parents were instantly on his back, biting him and tearing at his clothing. Many months later in Ruhengeri I saw that he still bore deep scars from the encounter on his legs and arms.

Charge anecdotes do the gorilla an injustice. Were it not for human encroachment into their terrain, the animals undoubtedly would have to charge only when defending their familial groups from intrusion by other gorillas. I remain deeply concerned about having habituated gorillas to human beings. This is one reason I do not habituate them to members of my African staff. Gorillas have known Africans only as poachers in the past. The second that it takes a gorilla to determine if an African is friend or foe is the second that might cost the animal its life from a spear, arrow, or bullet.

How ironic it is that probably less than a hundred men, armed with bows and arrows, spears or guns, have been allowed to plague the wildlife in the parklands that form the last stronghold for the mountain gorilla. The strongest counterstrategy against the abuse encroachers bestow upon the wildlife of the Virungas may be that of active conservation. Active conservation is a straightforward issue. It begins with providing personal incentive on a one-to-one basis with individual Africans, not only to take pride in their park but also to assume personally some of the responsibility toward the protection of their heritage. Given the incentive, active conservation is accomplished by very fundamental needs such as boots for the rangers' feet, decent clothing and raingear, ample food, and adequate wages. Thus equipped, hundreds of antipoacher patrols have set out from Karisoke into the heartland of the Virungas to cut traps, confiscate encroachers' weapons, and release newly trapped animals from snares. Active conservation within a steadily shrinking internationally designated sanctuary filled with poachers, traps, herdsmen, farmers, and beekeepers needs to be supplemented by Rwandese and Zairoise enforcement of anti-encroacher laws as well as severe penalties for the illegal sale of poached animals for their meat, skins, tusks, or for financial profits. Active conservation does not rule out any other long-term conservation approaches.

Theoretical conservation as a sole conservation effort is in marked contrast to active conservation. To an impoverished country such as Rwanda, an abstract rather than practical approach is more appealing. Theoretical conservation seeks to encourage growth in tourism by improving existing roads that circle the mountains of the Parc des Volcans, by renovating the park headquarters and tourists lodging and by the habituation of gorillas near the park boundaries for tourists to visit and photograph. Theoretical conservation is lauded highly by Rwandese government and park officials, who are understandably eager to see the Parc des Volcans gain international acclaim and to justify its economic existence in a land-scarce country, these efforts attract increasing numbers of sightseers to the Parc des Volcans. In 1980 alone, the park's revenue from tourism more than doubled over that received in 1979.

There is a failure to realize that the immediate needs of some 200 remaining mountain gorilla, and also of other Virunga wildlife now struggling for survival on a day-to-day basis, are not met by the long-term goals of theoretical conservation. Gorillas and the other park animals do not have time to wait. It takes only one trap, one bullet to kill a gorilla. For this reason it is mandatory that conservation efforts be actively concentrated on the immediate perils existing within the park. Next to these efforts, all others become theoretical. Educating the local populace to respect gorillas and working to attract tourism do not help the 242 remaining gorillas of the Virungas survive

for future generations of tourists to enjoy. Theoretical conservation has good long-term goals that needlessly ignore desperate immediate needs.

Far from the public's eye active conservation continues in the Parc des Volcans with a handful of dedicated people who work tirelessly behind the scenes to protect the park and its wildlife. One outstanding person who risked his position for what he believed, is Paulin Nkubili. As Rwandese Chef des Brigades, he inflicted strong penalties upon both buyers' and sellers' game illegally poached from the Parc des Volcans. By his actions, he also essentially eliminated the trophy market involving the sale of gorillas' heads and hands for souvenirs. There are some members of the Watutsi clan of Rutshema, a people who for generations grazed cattle illegally in the park, who themselves became active conservationists by leading antipoacher patrols in the Virungas. Paulin Nkubili, loyal members of the Karisoke Research Centre staff, and those of the patrols are each personally motivated in their unheralded efforts and rewarded only in the knowledge of their accomplishments. The hope for the future of the Virungas lies in the hands of just such individuals.

# KARISOKE FIELD IMPRESSIONS

# CHIMPS GRIEVE AS MUCH AS HUMANS DO:
## *Scientists Capture Group's Response to a Quiet Death*

### Elizabeth Weise

P ansy had a peaceful death. When the fifty something took to her bed, her son, daughter and an older friend gathered around her.

Moments after she died, they jostled her, then moved away from the death-bed. Finally, her daughter came back and laid down next to her mother's body but slept poorly. For the next five days, her son refused to set foot in the area where she had died.

A death surrounded by family and friends might not be remarkable, except that these were chimpanzees at the Blair Drummond Safari Park in Scotland, and this was the first time anyone had captured on video a chimpanzee group at the moment of a quiet death. "We were quite moved as we watched it unfold in real time," says James Anderson, a psychologist who studies primate behavior at the University of Stirling in Scotland.

The researchers publish an account of Pansy's death in today's edition of the journal *Current Biology*. Their account is paired with one describing the responses of two chimp mothers who lost babies in an outbreak of respiratory disease.

Anderson says researchers don't want to anthropomorphize the behavior, but the chimps' instinctive response to Pansy's death might be something that "predate(s) the religious or ritual significance we attach to our behaviors around death."

In many ways, it's not surprising, says Cheryl Knotts, a biological anthropologist at Boston University. It's possible to see the beginnings of many elements of human behaviors in chimpanzees and bonobos, such as tool use and communication.

These accounts "seem to show an attachment, a concern, for the dead or dying individual that is reminiscent of what we see in humans and possibly a precursor" to more elaborate awareness among humans, she says.

# CHIMPS GRIEVE AS MUCH AS HUMANS DO

A second article, by researchers observing a small chimpanzee colony in Bossou, Guinea, in Africa, describes how the two chimp mothers continued to carry and care for the mummified remains of their babies for two months and three weeks, respectively, after they died.

The carrying of dead infants occurs in many primate species, says John Mitani, a primatologist at the University of Michigan in Ann Arbor. "It's curious behavior, and we don't quite understand what's going on."

Dora Biro, one of the zoologists who observed the chimpanzee community, says the best explanation she can give is that the mother-infant bond is so strong that the mothers are programmed by natural selection to never let go of the infant. "She can't give up the infant's body because she knows she must look after it," she says.

"Chimps Grieve as Much as Humans Do," by Elizabeth Weise. USA TODAY, April 27, 2010, p. 7D. Reprinted with permission obtained via RightsLink.

# ARE WE IN ANTHROPODENIAL?

Frans de Waal

When guests arrive at the Yerkes Regional Primate Research Center in Georgia, where I work, they usually pay a visit to the chimpanzees. And often, when she sees them approaching the compound, an adult female chimpanzee named Georgia will hurry to the spigot to collect a mouthful of water. She'll then casually mingle with the rest of the colony behind the mesh fence, and not even the sharpest observer will notice anything unusual. If necessary, Georgia will wait minutes, with her lips closed, until the visitors come near. Then there will be shrieks, laughs, jumps—and sometimes falls—when she suddenly sprays them.

I have known quite a few apes that are good at surprising people, naive and otherwise. Heini Hediger, the great Swiss zoo biologist, recounts how he—being prepared to meet the challenge and paying attention to the ape's every move—got drenched by an experienced chimpanzee. I once found myself in a similar situation with Georgia; she had taken a drink from the spigot and was sneaking up to me. I looked her straight in the eye and pointed my finger at her, warning in Dutch, "I have seen you!" She immediately stepped back, let some of the water dribble from her mouth, and swallowed the rest. I certainly do not wish to claim that she understands Dutch, but she must have sensed that I knew what she was up to, and that I was not going to be an easy target.

Now, no doubt even a casual reader will have noticed that in describing Georgia's actions, I've implied human qualities such as intentions, the ability to interpret my own awareness, and a tendency toward mischief. Yet scientific tradition says I should avoid such language—I am committing the sin of anthropomorphism, of turning nonhumans into humans. The word comes from the Greek, meaning "human form," and it was the ancient Greeks who first gave the practice a bad reputation. They did not have chimpanzees in mind: the philosopher Xenophanes objected to Homer's poetry because it treated Zeus and the other gods as if they were people.

# ARE WE IN ANTHROPODENIAL?

How could we be so arrogant, Xenophanes asked, as to think that the gods should look like us? If horses could draw pictures, he suggested mockingly, they would no doubt make their gods look like horses.

Nowadays the intellectual descendants of Xenophanes warn against perceiving animals to be like ourselves. There are, for example, the behaviorists, who follow psychologist B. F. Skinner in viewing the actions of animals as responses shaped by rewards and punishments rather than the result of internal decision making, emotions, or intentions. They would say that Georgia was not "up to" anything when she sprayed water on her victims. Far from planning and executing a naughty plot, Georgia merely fell for the irresistible reward of human surprise and annoyance. Whereas any person acting like her would be scolded, arrested, or held accountable, Georgia is somehow innocent.

Behaviorists are not the only scientists who have avoided thinking about the inner life of animals. Some sociobiologists—researchers who look for the roots of behavior in evolution—depict animals as "survival machines" and "pre-programmed robots" put on Earth to serve their "selfish" genes. There is a certain metaphorical value to these concepts, but is has been negated by the misunderstanding they've created. Such language can give the impression that only genes are entitled to an inner life. No more delusively anthropomorphizing idea has been put forward since the pet-rock craze of the 1970s. In fact, during evolution, genes—a mere batch of molecules—simply multiply at different rates, depending on the traits they produce in an individual. To say that genes are selfish is like saying a snowball growing in size as it rolls down a hill is greedy for snow.

Logically, these agnostic attitudes toward a mental life in animals can be valid only if they're applied to our own species as well. Yet it's uncommon to find researchers who try to study human behavior as purely a matter of reward and punishment. Describe a person as having intentions, feelings, and thoughts and you most likely won't encounter much resistance. Our own familiarity with our inner lives overrules whatever some school of thought might claim about us. Yet despite this double standard toward behavior in humans and animals, modern biology leaves us no choice other than to conclude that we *are* animals. In terms of anatomy, physiology, and neurology we are really no

more exceptional than, say, an elephant or a platypus is in its own way. Even such presumed hallmarks of humanity as warfare, politics, culture, morality, and language may not be completely unprecedented. For example, different groups of wild chimpanzees employ different technologies—some fish for termites with sticks, others crack nuts with stones—that are transmitted from one generation to the next through a process reminiscent of human culture.

Given these discoveries, we must be very careful not to exaggerate the uniqueness of our species. The ancients apparently never gave much thought to this practice, the opposite of anthropomorphism, and so we lack a word for it. I will call it anthropodenial: a blindness to the human-like characteristics of other animals, or the animal-like characteristics of ourselves.

Those who are in anthropodenial try to build a brick wall to separate humans from the rest of the animal kingdom. They carry on the tradition of René Descartes, who declared that while humans possessed souls, animals were mere automatons. This produced a serious dilemma when Charles Darwin came along: If we descended from such automatons, were we not automatons ourselves? If not, how did we get to be so different?

Each time we must ask such a question, another brick is pulled out of the dividing wall, and to me this wall is beginning to look like a slice of Swiss cheese. I work on a daily basis with animals from which it is about as hard to distance yourself as from "Lucy," the famed 3.2-million-year-old fossil australopithecine. If we owe Lucy the respect of an ancestor, does this not force a different look at the apes? After all, as far as we can tell, the most significant difference between Lucy and modern chimpanzees is found in their hips, not their craniums.

As soon as we admit that animals are far more like our relatives than like machines, then anthropodenial becomes impossible and anthropomorphism becomes inevitable—and scientifically acceptable. But not *all* forms of anthropomorphism, of course. Popular culture bombards us with examples of animals being humanized for all sorts of purposes, ranging from education to entertainment to satire to propaganda. Walt Disney, for example, made us forget that Mickey is a mouse, and Donald a duck. George Orwell laid a cover of human societal ills over a population of livestock. I was once struck by an advertisement for an oil company that claimed its propane saved the environment, in which a grizzly bear enjoying a pristine landscape had his arm around his mate's shoulders. In fact, bears are nearsighted and do not form pair-bonds, so the image says more about our own behavior than theirs.

Perhaps that was the intent. The problem is, we do not always remember that, when used in this way, anthropomorphism can provide insight only into human affairs and not into the affairs of animals. When my book *Chimpanzee Politics* came out in France, in 1987, my publisher decided (unbeknownst to me) to put François Mitterrand and Jacques Chirac on the cover with a chimpanzee between them. I can only assume he wanted to imply that these politicians acted like "mere" apes. Yet by doing so he went completely against the whole point of my book, which was not to ridicule people but to show that chimpanzees live in complex societies full of alliances and power plays that in some ways mirror our own.

You can often hear similar attempts at anthropomorphic humor in the crowds that form around the monkey exhibit at a typical zoo. Isn't it interesting that antelopes, lions, and giraffes rarely elicit hilarity? But people who watch primates end up hooting and yelling, scratching themselves in exaggeration, and pointing at the animals while shouting, "I had to look twice, Larry. I thought it was you!" In my mind, the laughter reflects anthropodenial: it is a nervous reaction caused by an uncomfortable resemblance.

That very resemblance, however, can allow us to make better use of anthropomorphism, but for this we must view it as a means rather than an end. It should not be our goal to find some quality in an animal that is precisely equivalent to an aspect of our own inner lives. Rather, we should use the fact that we are similar to animals to develop ideas we can test. For example, after observing a group of chimpanzees at length, we begin to suspect that some individuals are attempting to "deceive" others—by giving false alarms to distract unwanted attention from the theft of food or from forbidden sexual activity. Once we frame the observation in such terms, we can devise testable predictions. We can figure out just what it would take to demonstrate deception on the part of chimpanzees. In this way, a speculation is turned into a challenge.

Naturally, we must always be on guard. To avoid making silly interpretations based on anthropomorphism, one must always interpret animal behavior in the wider context of a species' habits and natural history. Without experience with primates, one could imagine that a grinning rhesus monkey must be delighted, or that a chimpanzee running toward another with loud grunts must be in an aggressive mood. But primatologists know from many hours of observation that rhesus monkeys bare their teeth when intimidated, and that chimpanzees often grunt when they meet and embrace. In other words, a grinning rhesus monkey signals submission, and a chimpanzee's grunting often serves as a greeting. A careful observer may thus arrive at an informed anthropomorphism that is at odds with extrapolations from human behavior.

One must also always be aware that some animals are more like ourselves than others. The problem of sharing the experiences of organisms that rely on different senses is a profound one. It was expressed most famously by the philosopher Thomas Nagel when he asked, "What is it like to be a bat?" A bat perceives its world in pulses of reflected sound, something we creatures of vision would have a hard time imagining. Perhaps even more alien would be the experience of an animal such as the star-nosed mole. With 22 pink, writhing tentacles around its nostrils, it is able to feel microscopic textures on small objects in the mud with the keenest sense of touch of any animal on Earth.

Humans can barely imagine a star-nosed mole's *Umwelt*—a German term for the environment as perceived by the animal. Obviously, the closer a species is to us, the easier it is to enter its *Umwelt*. This is why anthropomorphism is not only tempting in the case of apes but also hard to reject on the grounds that we cannot know how they perceive the world. Their sensory systems are essentially the same as ours.

Last summer, an ape saved a three-year-old boy. The child, who had fallen 20 feet into the primate exhibit at Chicago's Brookfield Zoo, was scooped up and carried to safety by Binti Jua, an eight-year-old western lowland female gorilla. The gorilla sat down on a log in a stream, cradling the boy in her lap and patting his back, and then carried him to one of the exhibit doorways before laying him down and continuing on her way.

Binti became a celebrity overnight, figuring in the speeches of leading politicians who held her up as an example of much-needed compassion. Some scientists were less lyrical, however. They cautioned that Binti's motives might have been less noble than they appeared, pointing out that this gorilla had been raised by people and had been taught parental skills with a stuffed animal. The whole affair might have been one of a confused maternal instinct, they claimed.

The intriguing thing about this flurry of alternative explanations was that nobody would think of raising similar doubts when a person saves a dog hit by a car. The rescuer might have grown up around a kennel, have been praised for being kind to animals, have a nurturing personality, yet we would still see his behavior as an act of caring. Whey then, in Binti's case, was her background held against her? I am not saying that I know what went through Binti's head, but I do know that no one had prepared her for this kind of emergency and that it is unlikely that, with her own 17-month-old infant on her back, she was "maternally confused." How in the world could such a highly intelligent animal mistake a blond boy in sneakers and a red T-shirt for a juvenile gorilla? Actually, the biggest surprise was how surprised most people were. Students of ape behavior did not feel that Binti had done anything unusual. Jörg Hess, a Swiss gorilla expert, put it most bluntly, "The incident can be sensational only for people who don't know a thing about gorillas."

Binti's action made a deep impression mainly because it benefited a member of our own species, but in my work on the evolution of morality and empathy, I have encountered numerous instances of animals caring for one another. For example, a chimpanzee consoles a victim after a violent attack, placing an arm around him and patting his back. And bonobos (or pygmy chimpanzees) have been known to assist companions new to their quarters in zoos, taking them by the hand to guide them through the maze of corridors connecting parts of their building. These kinds of cases don't reach the newspapers but are consistent with Binti's assistance to the unfortunate boy and the idea that apes have a capacity for sympathy.

The traditional bulwark against this sort of cognitive interpretation is the principle of parsimony—that we must make as few assumptions as possible when trying to construct a scientific explanation, and that assuming an ape is capable of something like sympathy is too great a leap. But doesn't that same principle of parsimony argue against assuming a huge cognitive gap when the evolutionary distance between humans and apes is so small? If two closely related species

act in the same manner, their underlying mental processes are probably the same, too. The incident at the Brookfield Zoo shows how hard it is to avoid anthropodenial and anthropomorphism at the same time: in trying to avoid thinking of Binti as a human being, we run straight into the realization that Binti's actions make little sense if we refuse to assume intentions and feelings.

In the end we must ask: What kind of risk we are willing to take—the risk of underestimating animal mental life or the risk of overestimating it? There is no simple answer. But from an evolutionary perspective, Binti's kindness, like Georgia's mischief, is most parsimoniously explained in the same way we explain our own behavior—as the result of a complex, and familiar, inner life.

---

Frans de Waal is a professor of psychology at Emory University and research professor at the Yerkes Regional Primate Research Center in Atlanta. He is the author of several books, including *Chimpanzee Politics* and *Good Natured: The Origins of Right and Wrong in Humans and Other Animals*. His latest book, in collaboration with acclaimed wildlife photographer Frans Lanting, is *Bonobo: The Forgotten Ape*, published by the University of California Press (1997).

# SECTION III:
*Hominid Evolution*

# 9 *ARDIPITHECUS RAMIDUS*

## Ann Gibbons

*A rare 4.4-million-year-old skeleton has drawn back the curtain of time to reveal the surprising body plan and ecology of our earliest ancestors.*

Only a handful of individual fossils have become known as central characters in the story of human evolution. They include the first ancient human skeleton ever found, a Neandertal from Germany's Neander Valley; the Taung child from South Africa, which in 1924 showed for the first time that human ancestors lived in Africa; and the famous Lucy, whose partial skeleton further revealed a key stage in our evolution. In 2009, this small cast got a new member: Ardi, now the oldest known skeleton of a putative human ancestor, found in the Afar Depression of Ethiopia with parts of at least 35 other individuals of her species.

Ever since Lucy was discovered in 1974, researchers wondered what her own ancestors looked like and where and how they might have lived. Lucy was a primitive hominin, with a brain roughly the size of a chimpanzee's, but at 3.2 million years old, she already walked upright like we do. Even the earliest members of her species, *Australopithecus afarensis*, lived millions of years after the last common ancestor we shared with chimpanzees. The first act of the human story was still missing.

Now comes Ardi, a 4.4-million-year-old female who shines bright new light on an obscure time in our past. Her discoverers named her species *Ardipithecus ramidus*, from the Afar words for "root" and "ground," to describe a ground-living ape near the root of the human family tree. Although some hominins are even older, Ardi is by far the most complete specimen of such antiquity. The 125 pieces of her skeleton include most of the skull and teeth, as well as the pelvis, hands, arms, legs, and feet. (The 47-million-year-old fossil of the early primate called Ida is also remarkably complete, but she is not a direct ancestor to humans, as initially claimed during her debut this year.)

When the first fossils of Ardi's species were found in 1994, they were immediately recognized as the most important since Lucy. But the excitement was quickly tempered by Ardi's poor condition: The larger bones were crushed and brittle, and it took a multidisciplinary team 15 years to excavate Ardi, digitally remove distortions, and analyze her bones.

# ARDIPITHECUS RAMIDUS

Ardi's long-awaited skeleton was finally unveiled in 11 papers in print and online in October (*Science*, 2 October, pp. 60–106). Her discoverers proposed that she was a new kind of hominin, the family that includes humans and our ancestors but not the ancestors of other living apes. They say that Ardi's unusual anatomy was unlike that of living apes or later hominins, such as Lucy. Instead, Ardi reveals the ancient anatomical changes that laid the foundation for upright walking.

Not all paleoanthropologists are convinced that *Ar. ramidus* was our ancestor or even a hominin. But no one disputes the importance of the new evidence. Only a half-dozen partial skeletons of hominins older than 1 million years have ever been published. And having a skeleton rather than bits and pieces from different individuals not only provides a good look at the whole animal but also serves as a Rosetta stone to help decipher more fragmentary fossils. As the expected debate over Ardi's anatomy and relations to other primates begins, researchers agree that she and the other specimens of her species provide a wealth of new and surprising data on some of the most fundamental questions of human evolution: How can we identify the earliest members of the human family? How did upright walking evolve? What did our last common ancestor with chimpanzees look like? From now on, researchers asking those questions will refer to Ardi.

## Body of Evidence

Ardi's biggest surprise is that she was not transitional between *Australopithecus* and a common ancestor that looked like living chimpanzees and gorillas. Standing 120 centimeters tall, Ardi had a body and brain only slightly larger than a chimpanzee's, and she was far more primitive than Lucy. But she did not look like an African ape, or even much like the known fragments of more ancient apes.

When researchers studied her face and teeth, they found derived features that tie *Ardipithecus* to all later hominins, including Lucy's species and us. For example, Ardi's muzzle juts out less than a chimpanzee's does. Even males of her species lacked the large, sharp, daggerlike upper canines seen in chimpanzees. The base of her skull is short from front to back, as in upright walkers, rather than elongated, as in quadrupedal apes.

In addition, Ardi's pelvis convinced her discoverers that she did indeed walk upright—long the defining trait for being a member of the human family. The upper blades of Ardi's pelvis are shorter and broader than in living apes, lowering her center of gravity so she could balance on one leg at a time while walking, for example. But she didn't walk as well as humans or Lucy. Her pelvis was useful for both climbing and upright walking, making her a "facultative" biped, according to her discoverers.

Ardi's remarkably complete hand and foot bones add to this picture. Her wrist joints were not as stiff as those of African apes, and the bones of her palm were short, indicating that she did not knuckle-walk like chimpanzees or swing beneath tree branches, the discoverers say. Yet Ardi's foot was more rigid than a chimpanzee's, suggesting that it was an odd mosaic used for both upright walking on the ground and careful climbing and walking atop branches in the trees. Indeed, Ardi's long curving fingers and opposable big toe suggest she grasped tree branches.

If so, our ancestors began walking upright while still living primarily in a woodland rather than in more open, grassy terrain, as once believed. The international discovery team went to great lengths to reconstruct the scene where Ardi took her first steps, collecting 150,000 specimens of fossil plants and animals from Aramis and nearby. After using radiometric methods to tightly date the fossil-bearing sediments to 4.4 million years ago, the team concluded that Ardi lived on an ancient floodplain covered in sylvan woodlands, climbing among hackberry, fig, and palm trees, and coexisting with monkeys, kudu antelopes, and peafowl.

## Human Relations

At face value, Ardi is a hominin—if you define hominin on the basis of traits in the face, skull, and teeth. Many researchers who have read the descriptions of *Ardipithecus* or seen casts of the fossils agree on this. But since Lucy's discovery, the gold standard for identifying a hominin has been walking upright. Among primates, only humans and our closest relatives were habitual bipeds. On this point, Ardi stands on shakier ground.

The pelvis, which provides the pivotal evidence for upright walking, is fragmentary and crushed—parts of it have been called "Irish stew"—and outside researchers want to review its reconstruction. The discoverers note, however, that the interpretation of upright walking rests on traits in the foot and on the best-preserved portions of the original pelvis, not the reconstruction.

A few outside researchers who have already seen the cast of the pelvis agree that it shares some key traits with later hominins, such as the shape and size of a large opening known as the sciatic notch. Yet Ardi's hands and feet are so primitive that some researchers strongly question whether she really walked upright more often than other apes or was less able to climb and swing beneath branches. The next steps will be to further compare Ardi's bones with those of more ancient apes and to see how her unique anatomical features affected how she moved.

Many researchers also challenge the papers' forceful argument that Ardi reveals the basic body plan of the common ancestor of humans and chimpanzees. They point out that Ardi lived perhaps 1 million to 3 million years after that ancestor—plenty of time for evolutionary change. Some also question the social implications of *Ardipithecus* males' reduced canines, which the discovery team interprets as implying less male–male aggression than is seen in chimps.

The debate reveals how hard it is to identify upright walking in such an early hominin. Must Ardi walk upright like an australopithecine to be admitted to the human family? Or is it enough that she walked upright in an intermediate manner, if her face, skull, and canines align her with later protohumans? Ardi is already prompting some to ask whether habitual upright walking is essential to being a hominin. Perhaps some ancient apes became hominins head-first.

There's precedent for new hominin fossils provoking controversy and redefining what it means to be a member of the human family. Many thought a big brain and tool use emerged in concert with upright walking—until Lucy, with her chimp-sized brain, proved that upright walking came first.

As researchers ponder the definition of a hominin, they also wonder exactly where Ardi fits in our family tree. The discovery team suggested as one hypothesis that *Ardipithecus* gave rise to Lucy's genus *Australopithecus*, which is generally thought to have led to our own genus, *Homo*. But they also noted that Ardi could have been a side branch, an extinct lineage that was a sister species to our direct ancestors. As the study of Ardi widens to include new

collaborators, the team is granting requests to view the casts and will return to Aramis to search for more fossils.

In the year of the bicentennial of Darwin's birth, it seems fitting that researchers finally broke through the 4-million-year barrier to understanding our origins. Models for our earliest ancestors can now be informed by plenty of fresh data and at least one body of hard evidence.

*"Ardipithecus ramidus,"* by Ann Gibbons, SCIENCE, 18 December, 2009: Vol. 326, No. 5960 pp. 1598–1599. Reprinted with permission from *Science*, obtained via RightsLink.

# PALEOANTHROPOLOGY:
## *Candidate Human Ancestor from South Africa Sparks Praise and Debate*
### Michael Balter

*Australopithecus sediba makes its debut.*

"Dad, I found a fossil!"

Lee Berger glanced over at the rock his 9-year-old son, Matthew, was holding and figured the bone sticking out of it was probably that of an antelope, a common find in ancient South African rocks. But when Berger, a paleoanthropologist at the University of the Witwatersrand, Johannesburg, took a closer look, he recognized it as something vastly more important: the collar bone of an ancient hominin. Then he turned the block around and spotted a hominin lower jaw jutting out. "I couldn't believe it," he says.

Now on pages 195 and 205 of this issue of *Science*, Berger and his co-workers claim that these specimens, along with numerous other fossils found since 2008 in Malapa cave north of Johannesburg and dated as early as 2 million years ago, are those of a new species dubbed *Australopithecus sediba*. *Sediba* means "wellspring" in the Sesotho language, and Berger's team argues that the fossils have a mix of primitive features typical of australopithecines and more advanced characteristics typical of later humans. Thus, the team says, the new species may be the best candidate yet for the immediate ancestor of our genus, *Homo*.

That last claim is a big one, and few scientists are ready to believe it themselves just yet. But whether the new hominins are *Homo* ancestors or a side branch of late-surviving australopithecines, researchers agree that because of their completeness—including a skull and many postcranial bones—the fossils offer vital new clues to a murky area in human evolution. "This is a really remarkable find," says paleontologist Meave Leakey of the National Museums of Kenya in Nairobi, who thinks it's an australopithecine. "Very lovely specimens," says biological anthropologist William Kimbel of Arizona State University (ASU), Tempe, who thinks they are *Homo*.

Such different views of how to classify these fossils reflect a still-emerging debate over whether they are part of our own lineage or belong to a southern African side branch. The oldest *Homo* specimens are scrappy and enigmatic, leaving researchers unsure about the evolutionary steps between the australopithecines and *Homo*. Some think that the earliest fossils assigned to that genus, called *H. habilis* and *H. rudolfensis* and dated to as early as 2.3 million years ago, are really australopithecines. "The transition to *Homo* continues to be almost totally confusing," says paleoanthropologist Donald Johanson of ASU Tempe, who has seen the new fossils. So it is perhaps no surprise that the experts disagree over whether the new bones represent australopithecines or early *Homo*. And for now, at least, they don't seem to mind the uncertainty. "All new discoveries make things more confusing" at first, says anthropologist Susan Antón of New York University.

The finds stem from a project Berger embarked on in early 2008 with geologist Paul Dirks, now at James Cook University in Townsville, Australia, to identify new caves likely to hold hominin fossils. Malapa, just 15 kilometers northeast of famous hominin sites such as Sterkfontein, had been explored by lime miners in the early 20th century; they apparently threw the block that Matthew Berger found out of the cave. (Matthew was originally included as a co-author on one of the papers, but *Science*'s reviewers nixed that idea, Berger says.)

When Berger's team excavated inside the cave, it found more of that first individual, a nearly complete skull and a partial skeleton of a boy estimated to be 11 or 12 years old, plus an adult female skeleton, embedded in cave sediments. These fossils are reported in *Science*. The researchers also found bones of at least two other individuals, including an infant and another adult female, that are yet to be published.

Dirks enlisted several experts to help date the fossils. Labs in Bern, Switzerland, and Melbourne, Australia, independently performed uranium-lead radiometric dating, taken from cave deposits immediately below the fossils. They yielded dates of 2.024 million and 2.026 million years respectively, with maximum error margins of ±62,000 years. Paleomagnetic studies suggest that layers holding the fossils were deposited between 1.95 million and 1.78 million years ago, and animal bones found with the hominins were consistent with these dates.

The uranium-lead dating is "credible" and indicates that the fossils are no more than 2 million years old, says

geochronologist Paul Renne of the Berkeley Geochronology Center in California, citing the strong reputations of the Bern and Melbourne groups. But Renne regards the paleomagnetic work, which relies on correctly identifying ancient polarity reversals in Earth's magnetic field, as less convincing. The cave's stratigraphy might not be complete enough to formally rule out a much younger paleomagnetic signal for the fossils, he says. Geochemist Henry Schwarcz of McMaster University in Hamilton, Canada, notes that the team suggests that the hominin bodies might have been moved by river flows after they fell into the cave from holes in the earth above. If so, the fossils may not be tightly associated with the dated deposits below and above them, Schwarcz says. But Dirks rejects that suggestion, pointing out that the bones were partly articulated with each other, implying that they were buried soon after death.

For now, many researchers are accepting the dates and moving on to consider the team's hypothesis that *A. sediba* represents a new species transitional between australopithecines and early *Homo*. That idea fits with Berger's long-held—and controversial—view that *A. africanus*, rather than the earlier species to which "Lucy" belongs, *A. afarensis*, was the true ancestor of *Homo*. (Some of Berger's other past claims have sparked strong criticism, including a highly publicized 2008 report of small-bodied humans on Palau, which Berger thought might shed light on the tiny hobbits of Indonesia. But other researchers say the Palau bones belong to a normal-sized modern human population.)

The team's claims for *A. sediba* are based on its contention that the fossils have features found in both genera. On the australopithecine side, the hominin boy's brain, which the team thinks had reached at least 95% of adult size, is only about 420 cubic centimeters in volume, less than the smallest known *Homo* brain of about 510 cc. The small body size of both skeletons, a maximum of about 1.3 meters, is typical of australopithecines, as are the relatively long arms. The team says *A. sediba* most resembles *A. africanus*, which lived in South Africa between about 3.0 million and 2.4 million years ago and is the most likely ancestor for the new species.

But *A. sediba* differs from *A. africanus* in traits that also link it to *Homo*. Compared with other australopithecines, *A. sediba* has smaller teeth, less pronounced cheekbones, and a more prominent nose, as well as longer legs and changes in the pelvis similar to those seen in later *H. erectus*. This species, also known in Africa as *H. ergaster* and considered an ancestor of *H. sapiens*, first appears in Africa about 1.9 million years ago. Some features of *A. sediba*'s pelvis, such as the ischium (bottom portion), which is shorter than in australopithecines, "do look like they are tending more in a *Homo* direction," says Christopher Ruff, a biological anthropologist at Johns Hopkins Medical School in Baltimore, Maryland.

The claimed *Homo*-like features suggest to some people that the fossils belong in that genus rather than *Australopithecus*. "I would have been happier with a *Homo* designation," based on the small size of the teeth and also their detailed structure, such as the shape of their cusps, says Antón. "It's *Homo*," agrees Johanson, citing features such as the relative thinness of the hominin's lower jaw.

But others are unconvinced by the *Homo* argument. The characteristics shared by *A. sediba* and *Homo* are few and could be due to normal variation among australopithecines or because of the boy's juvenile status, argues Tim White, a paleoanthropologist at the University of California, Berkeley. These characters change as a hominin grows, and the features of a young australopithecine could mimic those of ancient adult humans. He and others, such as Ron Clarke of Witwatersrand, think the new fossils might represent a late-surviving version of *A. africanus* or a closely related sister species to it, and so will be chiefly informative about that lineage. "Given its late age and *Australopithecus*-grade anatomy, it contributes little to the understanding of the origin of genus *Homo*," says White.

Putting *A. sediba* into *Homo* would require "a major redefinition" of that genus, adds paleoanthropologist Chris Stringer of the Natural History Museum in London. At no earlier than 2 million years old, *A. sediba* is younger than *Homo*-looking fossils elsewhere in Africa, such as an upper jaw from Ethiopia and a lower jaw from Malawi, both dated to about 2.3 million years ago. Berger and his co-workers agree that the Malapa fossils themselves cannot be *Homo* ancestors but suggest that *A. sediba* could have arisen somewhat earlier, with the Malapa hominins being late-surviving members of the species.

The team thought long and hard about putting the fossils into *Homo* but decided that given the small brain and other features, the hominin was "australopithecine-grade," says team member Steven Churchill of Duke University in Durham, North Carolina. However they are classified, the Malapa finds "are important specimens in the conversation" about the origins of our genus, says Antón, and "will have to be considered in the solution."

"Candidate Human Ancestor from South Africa Sparks Praise and Debate," by Michael Balter, SCIENCE, 9 April 2010: Vol. 328, No. 5975 pp. 154–155. Reprinted with Permission from *Science*, obtained via RightsLink.

# PALEOANTHROPOLOGY

# GO NORTH, YOUNG HOMINID, AND BRAVE THE CHILLY WINTER WEATHER:

## *Stone Tools in England Hint at Early Arrival of Human Relatives*

**Bruce Bower**

*Excavations at a site in southeastern England indicate that hominids chilled out there a surprisingly long time ago.*

Discoveries at Happisburgh, situated on an eroding stretch of coastline near the city of Norwich, show that members of an as-yet-unidentified *Homo* species settled on the fringes of northern Europe's boreal forests at least 800,000 years ago, well before many scientists had assumed, say archaeologist Simon Parfitt of University College London and his colleagues.

Hominids repeatedly trekked to this northern locale, Parfitt's team reports in the July 8 *Nature*. In excavations from 2005 to 2008, the researchers found 78 palm-sized stones with intentionally sharpened edges in several sediment layers.

"We suspect these tools were made by the last dregs of a larger hominid population that had come when the area was warmer, but hung on and survived under challenging conditions as the climate cooled," says anthropologist and study coauthor Chris Stringer of the Natural History Museum in London.

Until half a dozen years ago, researchers thought that hominids reached northern Europe no earlier than 500,000 years ago, says Robin Dennell of the University of Sheffield in England. "Now it's anyone's guess when our earliest ancestors came this far north," he says.

Fossil finds show that hominids migrating out of Africa reached western Asia by 1.8 million years ago (SN: 5/13/00, p. 308) and Spain's Atapuerca Mountains as early as 1.2 million years ago (SN: 3/29/08, p. 196). Recent stone-tool finds at Pakefield, another site in southeastern England, indicate that hominids lived there 700,000 years ago (SN: 1/14/06, p. 29). Because the climate warmed briefly at that time, researchers proposed that hominids spread northward when temperatures rose and retreated south when the going got cold.

The Happisburgh finds hammer that hypothesis, Parfitt's team contends. An array of environmental clues—including remains of cold-adapted animals, insects and plants—excavated along with the stone tools indicate that hominids weathered chilly northern European winters.

# GO NORTH, YOUNG HOMINID...

Summer temperatures in Happisburgh were similar to or slightly warmer than those of today, the team estimates, but winters were probably at least 3 degrees Celsius cooler: "still miserable for those used to Mediterranean climes," write geochronologists Andrew Roberts and Rainer Grun of the Australian National University in Canberra in a comment published with the new report.

Happisburgh toolmakers lived just outside what is today a densely forested, frigid swath of northern Europe. Forest plants and animals dwindled during ancient winters, the scientists say. Crucially, though, geological analyses indicate that Happisburgh lay on an ancient course of the River Thames, near the North Sea and what was then a land bridge connecting southeastern England to continental Europe.

Ocean tides would have formed freshwater pools in the river and brought in marine life, such as the mollusks and barnacles whose shells have been unearthed at Happisburgh. Marshes on the river's floodplain would have attracted mammoths, rhinos and horses. Bones of such creatures have also been recovered in the area, which has been worked by fossil hunters for more than a century.

Soil at the site contains evidence of a previously dated reversal of Earth's magnetic field that provides a minimum age estimate of 780,000 years for the hominid finds. Excavated remains of extinct fossil plants and animals, combined with data on marine oxygen isotopes used in dating ancient climate shifts, narrow the timing of hominid visits to relatively warm periods either around 840,000 or 950,000 years ago.

No hominid fossils have turned up at Happisburgh. Toolmakers at the site may have been related to hominids that resided in Atapuerca 800,000 to 1.2 million years old ago, Stringer says. Discoverers of those remains assigned them to a species called *Homo antecessor*, which the team considered a precursor of European Neandertals and modern humans.

*Homo erectus* and small-bodied *Homo floresiensis* (SN: 5/8/10, p. 14) also existed at that time, but lived in Asia and Indonesia, too far to have reached Happisburgh, Stringer contends.

Although *H. antecessor* seems a good bet to have made the Happisburgh tools, the site has yet to yield evidence of controlled fire use, hunting or regular campsites—which would give clues to hominid behavior, Dennell says. "Were they tourists, migrants or colonists?" he asks. "We don't know."

Other potential hominid sites along a stretch of coastline that includes Happisburgh may help answer that question. "This area has the potential to be a British version of Olduvai Gorge," Stringer says.

Work at Tanzania's Olduvai Gorge since the 1930s has produced key hominid finds dating to as early as 1.8 million years ago.

# WHAT'S COOKING?

## The Economist

*The first of five reports from the annual meeting of the American Association for the Advancement of Science looks at the evolutionary role of cookery.*

You are what you eat, or so the saying goes. But Richard Wrangham, of Harvard University, believes that this is true in a more profound sense than the one implied by the old proverb. It is not just you who are what you eat but the entire human species. And with *Homo sapiens*, what makes the species unique in Dr Wrangham's opinion is that its food is so often cooked.

Cooking is a human universal. No society is without it. No one other than a few faddists tries to survive on raw food alone. And the consumption of a cooked meal in the evening, usually in the company of family and friends, is normal in every known society. Moreover, without cooking, the human brain (which consumes 20-25% of the body's energy) could not keep running. Dr Wrangham thus believes that cooking and humanity are coeval.

In fact, as he outlined to the American Association for the Advancement of Science (AAAS), in Chicago, he thinks that cooking and other forms of preparing food are humanity's "killer app": the evolutionary change that underpins all of the other—and subsequent—changes that have made people such unusual animals.

Humans became human, as it were, with the emergence 1.8m years ago of a species called *Homo erectus*. This had a skeleton much like modern man's—a big, brain-filled skull and a narrow pelvis and rib cage, which imply a small abdomen and thus a small gut. Hitherto, the explanation for this shift from the smaller skulls and wider pelvises of man's apelike ancestors has been a shift from a vegetable-based diet to a meat-based one. Meat has more calories than plant matter, the theory went. A smaller gut could therefore support a larger brain.

Dr Wrangham disagrees. When you do the sums, he argues, raw meat is still insufficient to bridge the gap. He points out that even modern "raw foodists," members of a town–dwelling, back-to-nature social movement, struggle to maintain their weight—and they have access to animals and plants that have been bred for the table. Pre-agricultural man confined to raw food would have starved.

# WHAT'S COOKING?

### Firelight

Start cooking, however, and things change radically. Cooking alters food in three important ways. It breaks starch molecules into more digestible fragments. It "denatures" protein molecules, so that their amino-acid chains unfold and digestive enzymes can attack them more easily. And heat physically softens food. That makes it easier to digest, so even though the stuff is no more calorific, the body uses fewer calories dealing with it.

In support of his thesis, Dr Wrangham, who is an anthropologist, has ransacked other fields and come up with an impressive array of material. Cooking increases the share of food digested in the stomach and small intestine, where it can be absorbed, from 50% to 95% according to work done on people fitted for medical reasons with collection bags at the ends of their small intestines. Previous studies had suggested raw food was digested equally well as cooked food because they looked at faeces as being the end product. These, however, have been exposed to the digestive mercies of bacteria in the large intestine, and any residual goodies have been removed from them that way.

Another telling experiment, conducted on rats, did not rely on cooking. Rather the experimenters ground up food pellets and then recompacted them to make them softer. Rats fed on the softer pellets weighed 30% more after 26 weeks than those fed the same weight of standard pellets. The difference was because of the lower cost of digestion. Indeed, Dr Wrangham suspects the main cause of the modern epidemic of obesity is not overeating (which the evidence suggests—in America, at least—is a myth) but the rise of processed foods. These are softer, because that is what people prefer. Indeed, the nerves from the taste buds meet in a part of the brain called the amygdala with nerves that convey information on the softness of food. It is only after these two qualities have been compared that the brain assesses how pleasant a mouthful actually is.

The archaeological evidence for ancient cookery is equivocal. Digs show that both modern humans and Neanderthals controlled fire in a way that almost certainly means they could cook, and did so at least 200,000 years ago. Since the last common ancestor of the two species lived more than 400,000 years ago (see following story) fire-control is probably at least as old as that, for they lived in different parts of the world, and so could not have copied each other.

Older alleged sites of human fires are more susceptible to other interpretations, but they do exist, including ones that go back to the beginning of *Homo erectus*. And traces of fire are easily wiped out, so the lack of direct evidence for them is no surprise. Instead, Dr Wrangham is relying on a compelling chain of logic. And in doing so he may have cast light not only on what made humanity, but on one of the threats it faces today.

"What's cooking?" THE ECONOMIST, 2/19/09, from reports by the American Association for the Advancement of Science. Reprinted with permission obtained via RightsLink.

# MODERN PEOPLE CARRY AROUND NEANDERTAL DNA, GENOME REVEALS:

*Team Uncovers Long-Sought Evidence of Interbreeding*

**Tina Hesman Saey**

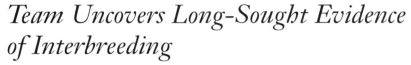

Some people don't just have a caveman mentality; they may actually carry a little relic of the Stone Age in their DNA. A new study of the Neandertal genome shows that humans and Neandertals interbred. The discovery comes as a big surprise to some researchers who have been searching for genetic evidence of human-Neandertal interbreeding for years and finding none.

About 1 to 4 percent of DNA in modern people from Europe and Asia was inherited from Neandertals, researchers report in the May 7 *Science*. "It's a small, but very real proportion of our ancestry," says study coauthor David Reich of the Broad Institute of MIT and Harvard in Cambridge, Mass. Comparisons of the human and Neandertal genomes are also revealing how humans evolved to become the sole living hominid species on the planet.

Neandertals formed a new branch on the hominid family tree more than 650,000 years ago and lived in Europe, the Middle East and western Asia before disappearing about 30,000 years ago. The new data, the team suggests, indicate that humans may not have replaced Neandertals, but rather assimilated them into the human gene pool.

"Neandertals are not totally extinct; they live on in some of us," says Svante Pääbo of the Max Planck Institute for Evolutionary Anthropology in Leipzig, Germany, and leader of the Neandertal genome project. He and other researchers involved in the effort to compile the complete genetic instruction book of Neandertals didn't expect to find that Neandertals had left a genetic legacy. Earlier analyses looking at only a small part of the genome had contradicted the notion that humans and Neandertals intermixed (SN Online: 8/7/08).

"We as a consortium came into this with a very, very strong bias against gene flow," Reich says. In fact, when announcing the completion of a rough draft of the Neandertal genome a year ago, the team said such genetic exchange was unlikely (SN: 3/14/09, p. 5). Several independent lines of evidence have now convinced the researchers otherwise.

# MODERN PEOPLE CARRY AROUND NEANDERTAL DNA

The result came as no surprise to some scientists, however. Archaeologists have described ancient skeletons from Europe that had characteristics of both early modern humans and Neandertals.

"After all these years the geneticists are coming to the same conclusions that some of us in the field of archaeology and human paleontology have had for a long time," says João Zilhão of the University of Bristol in England.

Pääbo's team re-created the Neandertal's genetic blueprints using DNA extracted from three bone fragments—each from a different Neandertal woman—found in a cave in Croatia. Then the researchers compared the genomes of these female Neandertals, who lived about 40,000 years ago, with those of five present-day humans from China, France, Papua New Guinea and southern and western Africa. The findings reveal that people of European and Asian ancestry carry Neandertal DNA.

Scientists were surprised to find that people from China and Papua New Guinea (places where Neandertals never lived) have just as much Neandertal ancestry as people from France. The group did not find traces of Neandertal heritage in the two African people studied. The result probably means that interbreeding took place about 50,000 to 80,000 years ago in the Middle East as humans began migrating out of Africa to colonize the rest of the world, Reich says.

It is not clear how extensive the inter-breeding was; the data are consistent with either a short period with a great deal of interbreeding or with a long period of little inter-breeding, says Richard "Ed" Green, a genome biologist now at the University of California, Santa Cruz and a coauthor of the new study.

Comparisons of the Neandertal genome to human and chimpanzee genetic sequences have led to some clues about recent human evolution. Neandertals "were not genetically very distinct from us," Pääbo says.

For example, the researchers were able to find only 73 proteins in which humans carry an amino acid different from the one found in Neandertals and chimpanzees. That means that few changes in proteins have taken place in the past few hundred thousand years of human evolution. Researchers don't know yet whether the changes in the proteins alter their function or give humans some survival advantage.

But some parts of the human genome clearly do produce an evolutionary advantage, the researchers say. If nothing of importance had happened in human evolution since humans and Neandertals diverged, differences would be spread evenly across the genome, Green says. Instead, the researchers found large swaths of the genome where humans have evolved differently from Neandertals and chimpanzees. The team identified 212 such regions where "selective sweeps" were likely to have happened, many of which include genes involved in brain function.

"These data are really a gold mine for understanding recent human evolution," Green says.

Since humans and Neandertals could interbreed, some people question whether the two groups are different hominid species. The question is still unsettled. Genealogically though, says anthropologist John Hawks of the University of Wisconsin–Madison, humans had a Neandertal great-great-great-great…grandfather. "It's impossible to talk about them as 'them' anymore," he says. "Neandertals are us."

**Cataloging differences:** Researchers have identified 73 proteins, some listed below, that have a form in humans that differs from the form found in Neandertals and chimpanzees.

| | |
|---|---|
| SPAG17 | Helps form the structure that makes sperm tails wiggle |
| PCD16 | A skin cell protein involved in wound healing |
| KR241 | Helps form the hair shaft |
| OR1K1 | An odor receptor |
| NLRX1 | Involved in regulating immune response |
| CALD1 | Helps regulate muscle contractions |

"Modern People Carry Around Neandertal DNA, Genome Reveals: Team Uncovers Long-Sought Evidence of Interbreeding," by Tina Hesman Saey, SCIENCE NEWS, June 5, 2010, Vol. 177, #12, pp.5–6. Reprinted with permission obtained via The Copyright Clearance Center.

# SECTION IV: *The Impact of Culture on Human Health and the Natural Environment*

# SECTION IV: *The Impact of Culture on Human Health...*

# 14 HUMAN CULTURE AS AN EVOLUTIONARY FORCE

Nicolas Wade

*As with any other species, human populations are shaped by the usual forces of natural selection, like famine, disease or climate. A new force is now coming into focus. It is one with a surprising implication—that for the last 20,000 years or so, people have inadvertently been shaping their own evolution.*

The force is human culture, broadly defined as any learned behavior, including technology. The evidence of its activity is the more surprising because culture has long seemed to play just the opposite role. Biologists have seen it as a shield that protects people from the full force of other selective pressures, since clothes and shelter dull the bite of cold and farming helps build surpluses to ride out famine.

Because of this buffering action, culture was thought to have blunted the rate of human evolution, or even brought it to a halt, in the distant past. Many biologists are now seeing the role of culture in a quite different light.

Although it does shield people from other forces, culture itself seems to be a powerful force of natural selection. People adapt genetically to sustained cultural changes, like new diets. And this interaction works more quickly than other selective forces, "leading some practitioners to argue that gene-culture co-evolution could be the dominant mode of human evolution," Kevin N. Laland and colleagues wrote in the February issue of *Nature Reviews Genetics*. Dr. Laland is an evolutionary biologist at the University of St. Andrews in Scotland.

The idea that genes and culture co-evolve has been around for several decades but has started to win converts only recently. Two leading proponents, Robert Boyd of the University of California–Los Angeles, and Peter J. Richerson of the University of California–Davis, have argued for years that genes and culture were intertwined in shaping human evolution. "It wasn't like we were despised, just kind of ignored," Dr. Boyd said. But in the last few years, references by other scientists to their writings have "gone up hugely," he said.

The best evidence available to Dr. Boyd and Dr. Richerson for culture being a selective force was the lactose tolerance found in many northern Europeans. Most people switch off the gene that digests the lactose in milk shortly after they are weaned, but in northern Europeans—the descendants of an ancient cattle-rearing culture that emerged in the region some 6,000 years ago—the gene is kept switched on in adulthood.

Lactose tolerance is now well recognized as a case in which a cultural practice—drinking raw milk—has caused an evolutionary change in the human genome. Presumably the extra nutrition was of such great advantage that adults able to digest milk left more surviving offspring, and the genetic change swept through the population.

This instance of gene-culture interaction turns out to be far from unique. In the last few years, biologists have been able to scan the whole human genome for the signatures of genes undergoing selection. Such a signature is formed when one version of a gene becomes more common than other versions because its owners are leaving more surviving offspring. From the evidence of the scans, up to 10 percent of the genome—some 2,000 genes—shows signs of being under selective pressure.

These pressures are all recent, in evolutionary terms—most probably dating from around 10,000 to 20,000 years ago, in the view of Mark Stoneking, a geneticist at the Max Planck Institute for Evolutionary Anthropology in Leipzig, Germany. Biologists can infer the reason for these selective forces from the kinds of genes that are tagged by the genome scans. The roles of most of the 20,000 or so genes in the human genome are still poorly understood, but all can be assigned to broad categories of likely function depending on the physical structure of the protein they specify.

By this criterion, many of the genes under selection seem to be responding to conventional pressures. Some are involved in the immune system, and presumably became more common because of the protection they provided against disease. Genes that cause paler skin in Europeans or Asians are probably a response to geography and climate.

But other genes seem to have been favored because of cultural changes. These include many genes involved in diet and metabolism and presumably reflect the major shift in diet that occurred in the transition from foraging to agriculture that started about 10,000 years ago.

Amylase is an enzyme in the saliva that breaks down starch. People who live in agrarian societies eat more starch and have extra copies of the amylase gene compared with people who live in societies that depend on hunting or fishing. Genetic changes that enable lactose tolerance have been detected not just in Europeans but also in three African pastoral societies. In each of the four cases, a different mutation is involved, but all have the same result—that of preventing the lactose-digesting gene from being switched off after weaning.

Many genes for taste and smell show signs of selective pressure, perhaps reflecting the change in foodstuffs as people moved from nomadic to sedentary existence. Another group under pressure is that of genes that affect the growth of bone. These could reflect the declining weight of the human skeleton that seems to have accompanied the switch to settled life, which started some 15,000 years ago.

A third group of selected genes affects brain function. The role of these genes is unknown, but they could have changed in response to the social transition as people moved from small hunter-gatherer groups a hundred strong to villages and towns inhabited by several thousand, Dr. Laland said. "It's highly plausible that some of these changes are a response to aggregation, to living in larger communities," he said.

Though the genome scans certainly suggest that many human genes have been shaped by cultural forces, the tests for selection are purely statistical, being based on measures of whether a gene has become more common. To verify that a gene has indeed been under selection, biologists need to perform other tests, like comparing the selected and unselected forms of the gene to see how they differ.

Dr. Stoneking and his colleagues have done this with three genes that score high in statistical tests of selection. One of the genes they looked at, called the EDAR gene, is known to be involved in controlling the growth of hair. A variant form of the EDAR gene is very common in East Asians and Native Americans, and is probably the reason that these populations have thicker hair than Europeans or Africans.

Still, it is not obvious why this variant of the EDAR gene was favored. Possibly thicker hair was in itself an advantage, retaining heat in Siberian climates. Or the trait could have become common through sexual selection, because people found it attractive in their partners.

A third possibility comes from the fact that the gene works by activating a gene regulator that controls the immune system as well as hair growth. So the gene could have been favored because it conferred protection against some disease, with thicker hair being swept along as a side effect. Or all three factors could have been at work. "It's one of the cases we know most about, and yet there's a lot we don't know," Dr. Stoneking said.

The case of the EDAR gene shows how cautious biologists have to be in interpreting the signals of selection seen in the genome scans. But it also points to the potential of the selective signals for bringing to light salient events in human prehistory as modern humans dispersed from the ancestral homeland in northeast Africa and adapted to novel environments. "That's the ultimate goal," Dr. Stoneking said. "I come from the anthropological perspective, and we want to know what the story is."

With archaic humans, culture changed very slowly. The style of stone tools called the Oldowan appeared 2.5 million years ago and stayed unchanged for more than a million years. The Acheulean stone tool kit that succeeded it lasted for 1.5 million years. But among behaviorally modern humans, those of the last 50,000 years, the tempo of cultural change has been far brisker. This raises the possibility that human evolution has been accelerating in the recent past under the impact of rapid shifts in culture.

Some biologists think this is a possibility, though one that awaits proof. The genome scans that test for selection have severe limitations. They cannot see the signatures of ancient selection, which get washed out by new mutations, so there is no base line by which to judge whether recent natural selection has been greater than in earlier times. There are also likely to be many false positives among the genes that seem favored.

But the scans also find it hard to detect weakly selected genes, so they may be picking up just a small fraction of the recent stresses on the genome. Mathematical models of gene-culture interaction suggest that this form of natural selection can be particularly rapid. Culture has become a force of natural selection, and if it should prove to be a major one, then human evolution may be accelerating as people adapt to pressures of their own creation.

"Human Culture as an Evolutionary Force," by Nicolas Wade, NEW YORK TIMES. March 2, 2010. Reprinted with permission obtained via RightsLink.

# HUMAN CULTURE AS AN EVOLUTIONARY FORCE

# DID EARLY MAN TURN THE OUTBACK INTO A BARREN DESERT?

Kate Ravilous

Once upon a time, Australia had a lush, green interior where grazing animals roamed, shrubs grew and the rain fell. Then, about 55,000 years ago, man arrived and started hunting the animals and burning the vegetation; ultimately, he drove the rain away and turned Australia's interior into the harsh, red, desert landscape that we see today.

There is no doubt that Australia's environment and climate has changed dramatically, but was man responsible? Gifford Miller, from the University of Colorado at Boulder, thinks so, and he and his colleagues have discovered convincing evidence to back up their theory.

The story starts at Lake Eyre, a huge salt flat covering one-sixth of Australia's landmass. Miller has been working with John Magee, of the Australian National University in Canberra, to drill down through the layers of mud, sand and salt at the site to uncover Lake Eyre's past. Going back 125,000 years, they have found that it used to be a vast freshwater lake, covering 35,000 square kilometers—an area the size of Taiwan. Rains used to swell the lake every year, following the patterns of the Australian monsoon. Then, about 14,000 years ago, "the monsoon stopped penetrating into the interior of Australia and Lake Eyre started to turn into a salt lake, like it is today," says Miller.

While he was looking for reasons as to why the monsoon could have failed, Miller discovered that the Australian environment had suffered other dramatic changes in the past. "About 50,000 years ago, some 60 different species of animal went extinct," he says. Miller's work focused on the demise of an ostrich-sized flightless bird called Genyornis newtoni. Measuring amino acids in the fossil eggshells of these birds and using radiocarbon dating, Miller and his colleagues found that Genyornis suddenly disappeared about 50,000 years ago. Meanwhile, other scientists have recorded that a host of other creatures, including a giant horned tortoise (the size of a small car) and a hippopotamus-sized relative of the wombat, were also snuffed out.

And animals were not the only ones to suffer. Pollen records suggest that many species of tree also vanished at this point. "Some of the most fire-sensitive plants, such as rainforest gynmosperms [whose seeds are not encased and thus protected from fire], disappear and never come back," says Miller. The evidence was circumstantial, but Miller became suspicious that all these sudden environmental changes were

# DID EARLY MAN TURN THE OUTBACK INTO A BARREN DESERT?

linked. He believes that early man may have pushed the natural balance too far by burning large areas of vegetation on a regular basis. The burning was probably used to hunt animals, promote new plant growth and exchange signals, but eventually it changed the environment irreparably. As well as burning plants and forcing animals to extinction, Miller thinks that man may be indirectly responsible for the monsoon failure—by removing the vegetation that sucked the rain into Australia's interior.

Miller and his colleagues have been looking at the link between Australia's vegetation and its climate, and using climate models to better understand the pattern of Australia's monsoons. Matching up pollen records with the Lake Eyre data has indicated that vegetation and climate used to be strongly linked. "Prior to 50,000 years ago, the vegetation beat to the same rhythm as the monsoon," says Miller. The lake data shows that Australia's monsoons followed processional cycles, related to the tilting of the Earth as it spins on its axis. Over a 22,000-year period, the Australian monsoon swung from being a deluge to a drizzle and back again. Similarly, the vegetation swung from being dominated by lush rainforest to being made up of higher proportions of shrubby plants and grass, and back again.

"The earliest humans arrived in Australia about 55,000 years ago, at the tail end of one of the stronger monsoon periods. There would have been lots of animals and plenty of green plants," says Miller. But that didn't last. By 45,000 years ago, Lake Eyre sediments show that the monsoon entered its weaker phase and became more of a dribble. At the same time, the Earth entered an ice age, making the planet cold and dry. It wasn't until about 14,000 years ago that the ice retreated and the monsoon rains started again. But, unlike on previous occasions, the strong monsoon rains never returned to the Australian interior. "We would have expected the climate to stay quite dry until about 14,000 years ago, but then the heavy monsoon should have reappeared," says Miller. Instead, the Lake Eyre sediments show that the interior of Australia continued to remain dry.

Using general circulation models (GCMs—climate simulators), Miller and his colleagues have been testing how sensitive the Australian monsoon is to changes in vegetation. They have found that plants appear to be the key to holding on to monsoon rainfall. When the model is run with vegetation covering the Australian interior, it gets twice the rainfall compared with a model run with no vegetation. "The GCM suggests that rainfall in the

interior would be about 600mm per year when trees and plants cover the ground, compared with about 300mm per year when the ground is bare," Miller says.

Vegetation is likely to be important because it helps to recycle the rain via evaporation and transpiration. "Plants collect moisture and hold onto it. Without any vegetation the rain either evaporates, or sinks into the ground and disappears," explains Miller. Trees also add "surface roughness" to a landscape, which is thought to promote convection and to encourage rain-cloud formation. If Australia's earliest human inhabitants burnt enough vegetation, Miller believes that this could have tipped the balance and prevented the monsoon rains from reaching the interior.

Today, northern Australia still receives an annual monsoon, dousing cities like Darwin with more than 1,600mm of rain a year. The GCM models have shown that Australia's monsoon is connected to the northern-hemisphere climate and the Asian monsoon. "Early man didn't have enough influence to affect the global monsoon pattern, but it appears that localized burning was enough to produce a continental-scale change in the water balance and climate," says Miller.

It is unlikely that we can turn the clock back for Australia. In principle, trees could be planted to entice the moisture back, but thousands of years of desert weathering has left Australian soil very low in nutrients, making it almost impossible for trees to get a grasp again. "Physics is working against us right now. Perhaps we could try planting in another 11,000 years, when we are in a strong monsoon period again," says Miller.

If Miller and his colleagues are right about Australia's past, it provides a sobering lesson. Rainforest is being felled all over the world at an unprecedented rate and ecosystems pushed way out of kilter. What kind of effect will this have on the world's climate? Are we leaving a legacy to future generations of desert landscapes and unpredictable rainfall?

# 16 HOW PREHISTORIC FARMERS SAVED US FROM NEW ICE AGE

Robin McKie

Ancient man saved the world from a new Ice Age. That is the startling conclusion of climate researchers who say man-made global warming is not a modern phenomenon and has been going on for thousands of years.

Prehistoric farmers who slashed down trees and laid out the first rice paddies and wheat fields triggered major alterations to levels of greenhouse gases such as methane and carbon dioxide in the atmosphere, they say.

As a result, global temperatures—which were slowly falling around 8,000 years ago—began to rise. "Current temperatures would be well on the way toward typical glacial temperatures, had it not been for the greenhouse gas contributions from early farming practices," says Professor William Ruddiman of Virginia University.

The theory, based on studies of carbon dioxide and methane samples taken from Antarctic ice cores, is highly controversial—a point acknowledged by Ruddiman. "Global warming skeptics could cite my work as evidence that human-generated greenhouse gases played a beneficial role for several thousand years by keeping the Earth's climate more hospitable than it would otherwise have been," he states in the current issue of *Scientific American*.

"However, others might counter that, if so few humans with relatively primitive technologies were able to alter the course of climate so significantly, then we have reason to be concerned about the current rise of greenhouse gases to unparalleled concentrations at unprecedented rates."

Elaborating on his theory, Ruddiman said: "Rice paddies flooded by irrigation generate methane for the same reason that natural wetlands do—vegetation decomposes in the stagnant water. Methane is also released as farmers burn grasslands," Ruddiman points out.

Similarly, the cutting down of forests had a major effect. "Whether the fallen trees were burnt or left to rot, their carbon would soon have been oxidized and ended up in the atmosphere as carbon dioxide."

Computer models of the climate made by scientists at the University of Wisconsin-Madison suggest this rise in carbon dioxide and methane would have had a profound effect on Earth: without man's intervention, our planet would be 2° cooler than it is now, and spreading ice caps and glaciers would affect much of the world.

The idea that ancient farming may have had an impact on Earth's climate was given a cautious welcome by Professor Paul Valdes, an expert on ancient climate change based at Bristol University.

"This is a very interesting idea," he told *The Observer*. "However, there are other good alternative explanations to explain the fluctuations that we see in temperature and greenhouse gas levels at this time. For example, other gases interact with methane and carbon dioxide in the atmosphere and changes in levels of these could account for these increases in greenhouse gases."

# GROWING OBESITY INCREASES PERILS OF CHILDBIRTH

### Anemona Hartocollis

As Americans have grown fatter over the last generation, inviting more heart disease, diabetes and premature deaths, all that extra weight has also become a burden in the maternity ward, where babies take their first breath of life.

About one in five women are obese when they become pregnant, meaning they have a body mass index of at least 30, as would a 5-foot-5 woman weighing 180 pounds, according to researchers with the federal Centers for Disease Control and Prevention. And medical evidence suggests that obesity might be contributing to record-high rates of Caesarean sections and leading to more birth defects and deaths for mothers and babies.

Hospitals, especially in poor neighborhoods, have been forced to adjust. They are buying longer surgical instruments, more sophisticated fetal testing machines and bigger beds. They are holding sensitivity training for staff members and counseling women about losing weight, or even having bariatric surgery, before they become pregnant.

At Maimonides Medical Center in Brooklyn, where 38 percent of women giving birth are obese, Patricia Garcia had to be admitted after she had a stroke, part of a constellation of illnesses related to her weight, including diabetes and weak kidneys.

At seven months pregnant, she should have been feeling the thump of tiny feet against her belly. But as she lay flat in her hospital bed, doctors buzzing about, trying to stretch out her pregnancy day by precious day, Ms. Garcia, who had recently weighed in at 261 pounds, said she was too numb from water retention to feel anything.

On May 5, 11 weeks shy of her due date, a sonogram showed that the baby's growth was lagging, and an emergency Caesarean was ordered.

# GROWING OBESITY INCREASES PERILS OF CHILDBIRTH

She was given general anesthesia because her bulk made it hard to feel her spine to place a local anesthetic. Dr. Betsy Lantner, the obstetrician on call, stood on a stool so she could reach over Ms. Garcia's belly. A flap of fat covered her bikini line, so the doctor had to make a higher incision. In an operation where every minute counted, it took four or five minutes, rather than the usual one or two, to pull out a 1-pound 11-ounce baby boy.

Studies have shown that babies born to obese women are nearly three times as likely to die within the first month of birth than women of normal weight, and that obese women are almost twice as likely to have a stillbirth.

About two out of three maternal deaths in New York State from 2003 to 2005 were associated with maternal obesity, according to the state-sponsored Safe Motherhood Initiative, which is analyzing more recent data.

Obese women are also more likely to have high blood pressure, diabetes, anesthesia complications, hemorrhage, blood clots and strokes during pregnancy and childbirth, data shows.

The problem has become so acute that five New York City hospitals—Beth Israel Medical Center and Mount Sinai Medical Center in Manhattan, Maimonides in Brooklyn and Montefiore Medical Center and Bronx-Lebanon Hospital Center in the Bronx—have formed a consortium to figure out how to handle it. They are supported by their malpractice insurer and the United Hospital Fund, a research group.

One possibility is to create specialized centers for obese women. The centers would counsel them on nutrition and weight loss, and would be staffed to provide emergency Caesarean sections and intensive care for newborns, said Dr. Adam P. Buckley, an obstetrician and patient safety expert at Beth Israel Hospital North who is leading the group.

Very obese women, or those with a B.M.I. of 35 or higher, are three to four times as likely to deliver their first baby by Caesarean section as first-time mothers of normal weight, according to a study by the Consortium on Safe Labor of the National Institutes of Health.

While doctors are often on the defensive about whether Caesarean sections, which carry all the risks of surgery,

are justified, Dr. Howard L. Minkoff, the chairman of obstetrics at Maimonides, said doctors must weigh those concerns against the potential complications from vaginal delivery in obese women. Typically, these include failing to progress in labor; diabetes in the mother, which can lead to birth complications; and difficulty monitoring fetal distress. "With obese women we are stuck between Scylla and Charybdis," Dr. Minkoff said.

But even routine care, like finding a vein to take blood, can be harder through layers of fatty tissue.

And equipment can be a problem. Dr. Janice Henderson, an obstetrician for high-risk pregnancies at Johns Hopkins in Baltimore, described a recent meeting where doctors worried that the delivery room table might collapse under the weight of an obese patient.

At Maimonides, the perinatal unit threw away its old examining tables and replaced them with wider, sturdier ones. It bought ultrasound machines that make lifelike three-dimensional images early in pregnancy, when the fetus is still low in the uterus and less obscured by fat, but also less developed and thus harder to diagnose clearly. "You really need to use the best equipment, which is more expensive," said Dr. Shoshana Haberman, the director of perinatal services.

Many experienced obstetricians complain that as Americans have grown larger, the perception of what constitutes obesity has shifted, leading to some complacency among doctors. At UMass Memorial Medical Center in Worcester, Mass., Dr. Tiffany A. Moore Simas, the associate director of the residency program in obstetrics, demands that residents calculate B.M.I. as a routine part of prenatal treatment. "It's one of my siren songs," Dr. Moore Simas said, "because we are very bad at eyeballing people."

Dr. Haberman said there was obesity in her own family, and she had seen how hurtful even professionals could be. "We as a society have issues with the perception of obesity; anatomically, you get turned off," she said.

So she was sympathetic to Ms. Garcia, making sure she got a room with a window, and calling to check on her after hours.

Ms. Garcia, 38, a former school bus dispatcher, is 5 feet tall. She said she had tried diets, weight-watching groups and joining a gym. She was 195 pounds before her pregnancy (B.M.I., 38) and ballooned to 261 pounds, which she attributed to water weight and inactivity.

"I'm the smallest one in my family," she said. Her older brother weighed more than 700 pounds before having gastric bypass surgery.

She wiped tears away as she confessed that she worried that she might die and leave her baby without a mother.

At Ms. Garcia's stage of pregnancy, every day in the womb was good for the baby but bad for the mother, Dr. Minkoff said. "She's making a heroic decision to put her own self in peril for the sake of the child," he said.

She survived, but was dismayed by the size of her son, Josiah Patrick, who had to be put on a breathing machine. At first she could see him only by remote video. But after a month, Josiah was off the ventilator, taking 15 milliliters of formula and had smiled at his mother, and doctors said he was where he should be developmentally for a preemie his age.

The hospital estimated that the cost of caring for the mother and baby would be more than $200,000, compared with $13,000 for a normal delivery.

Ms. Garcia promised Dr. Minkoff that she would lose weight and see her baby graduate from college. "I'm going on a strict, strict, strict diet," she said. "I'm not going through this again."

**"Growing Obesity Increases Perils of Childbirth" by Anemona Hartocollis, NEW YORK TIMES, June 5, 2010. Reprinted with permission obtained via RightsLink.**

# 18 FACING THE CONSEQUENCES

## The Economist

*Global action is not going to stop climate change.*
*The world needs to look harder at how to live with it.*

On November 29th representatives of countries from around the world will gather in Cancun, Mexico, for the first high-level climate talks since those in Copenhagen last December. The organisers hope the meeting in Mexico, unlike the one in Denmark, will be unshowy but solid, leading to decisions about finance, forestry and technology transfer that will leave the world better placed to do something about global warming. Incremental progress is possible, but continued deadlock is likelier. What is out of reach, as at Copenhagen, is agreement on a plausible programme for keeping climate change in check.

The world warmed by about 0.7°C in the 20th century. Every year in this century has been warmer than all but one in the last (1998, since you ask). If carbon-dioxide levels were magically to stabilise where they are now (almost 390 parts per million, 40% more than before the industrial revolution) the world would probably warm by a further half a degree or so as the ocean, which is slow to change its temperature, caught up. But $CO_2$ levels continue to rise. Despite 20 years of climate negotiation, the world is still on an emissions trajectory that fits pretty easily into the "business as usual" scenarios drawn up by the Intergovernmental Panel on Climate Change (IPCC).

The Copenhagen accord, a non-binding document which was the best that could be salvaged from the summit, talks of trying to keep the world less than 2°C warmer than in pre-industrial times—a level that is rather arbitrarily seen as the threshold for danger. Many countries have, in signing the accord, promised actions that will or should reduce carbon emissions. In the World Energy Outlook, recently published by the International Energy Agency, an assessment of these promises forms the basis of a "new policies scenario" for the next 25 years. According to the IEA, the scenario puts the world on course to warm by 3.5°C by 2100. For comparison, the difference in global mean temperature between the pre-industrial age and the ice ages was about 6°C.

93

The IEA also looked at what it might take to hit a two-degree target; the answer, says the agency's chief economist, Fatih Birol, is "too good to be believed." Every signatory of the Copenhagen accord would have to hit the top of its range of commitments. That would provide a worldwide rate of decarbonisation (reduction in carbon emitted per unit of GDP) twice as large in the decade to come as in the one just past: 2.8% a year, not 1.4%. Mr. Birol notes that the highest annual rate on record is 2.5%, in the wake of the first oil shock.

But for the two-degree scenario 2.8% is just the beginning; from 2020 to 2035 the rate of decarbonisation needs to double again, to 5.5%. Though they are unwilling to say it in public, the sheer improbability of such success has led many climate scientists, campaigners and policymakers to conclude that, in the words of Bob Watson, once the head of the IPCC and now the chief scientist at Britain's Department for Environment, Food and Rural Affairs, "Two degrees is a wishful dream."

The fight to limit global warming to easily tolerated levels is thus over. Analysts who have long worked on adaptation to climate change—finding ways to live with scarcer water, higher peak temperatures, higher sea levels and weather patterns at odds with those under which today's settled patterns of farming developed—are starting to see their day in the uncomfortably hot sun. That such measures cannot protect everyone from all harm that climate change may bring does not mean that they should be ignored. On the contrary, they are sorely needed.

## Public Harms

Many of these adaptations are the sorts of thing—moving house, improving water supply, sowing different seeds—that people will do for themselves, given a chance. This is one reason why adaptation has not been the subject of public debate in the same way as reductions in greenhouse-gas emissions from industry and deforestation have. But even if a lot of adaptation will end up being done privately, it is also a suitable issue for public policy.

For a start, some forms of adaptation—flood barriers, for instance—are clearly public goods, best supplied through collective action. Adaptation will require redistribution, too. Some people and communities are too poor to adapt on their own; and if emissions caused by the consumption of the rich imposes adaptation costs on the poor, justice demands recompense.

Furthermore, policymakers' neat division of the topic of climate change into mitigation, impact and adaptation is too simplistic. Some means of adaptation can also act as mitigation; a farming technique which helps soil store moisture better may well help it store carbon too. Some forms of adaptation will be hard to distinguish from the sort of impact you would rather avoid. Mass migration is a good way of adapting if the alternative is sitting still and starving; to people who live where the migrants turn up it may look awfully like an unwelcome impact.

Its frequently private and slightly blurry nature is not the only reason why adaptation has been marginalised. The green pressure groups and politicians who have driven the debate on climate change have often been loth to see attention paid to adaptation, on the ground that the more people thought about it, the less motivated they would be to push ahead with emissions reduction. Talking about adaptation was for many years like farting at the dinner table, says an academic who has worked on adaptation over the past decade. Now that the world's appetite for emissions reduction has been revealed to be chronically weak, putting people off dinner is less of a problem.

Another reason for taking adaptation seriously is that it is necessary now. Events such as this year's devastating floods in Pakistan make it obvious that the world has not adapted to the climate it already has, be it man-made or natural. Even if the climate were not changing, there would be two reasons to worry about its capacity to do more harm than before. One is that it varies a lot naturally and the period over which there are good global climate records is short compared with the time scale on which some of that variability plays out. People thus may be ignoring the worst that today's climate can do, let alone tomorrow's. The other is that more lives, livelihoods and property are at risk, even if hazards do not change, as a result of economic development, population growth and migration to coasts and floodplains.

## The Three-Degree Difference

In a late 21st-century world 3°C warmer than the pre-industrial norm, what changes are most marked? Start with the coldest bits. Arctic summer sea ice goes, allowing more shipping and mining, removing a landscape of which indigenous peoples were once an integral part. Permafrost warms up, and infrastructure built on it founders. Most mountain glaciers shrink; some disappear. Winter snows melt more quickly, and the risks of spring floods and summer water shortages on the rivers they feed increase.

Sea level rises, though by how much is hard to say. Some of the rise will be predictable, in that oceans expand as they get warmer. Some, though, will depend on the behavior of the Greenland and West Antarctic ice caps, which cannot be predicted with any certainty. Less than half a metre by 2100 would be a lucky break; a metre-plus is possible; more than two is very unlikely, but possible later.

Even as the waters rise, many coasts will be sinking because of the subsidence that follows as cities suck up ground-water. Deltas are doubly damned, since any subsidence is often coupled with a lessened supply of replenishing sediment, which is often trapped upstream by irrigation, hydropower production and flood-control projects. One estimate puts 8.7m more people at risk of flooding in deltas by 2050 if sea level follows current trends.

Tropical cyclones, which account for much of the damage the sea does to the land, may become less frequent. But the share of the most destructive—category 4 and category 5 hurricanes—seems likely to increase. And bigger storms do disproportionately greater damage.

In warmer oceans, coral bleaching triggered by tempera-ture stress will be more common. This is bad for fishing and tourism but not necessarily fatal to all the reefs: bleached reefs may be recolonised by new corals. Reefs may also face damage from ocean acidification, an effect of higher $CO_2$ levels rather than of warming, as may other ecosystems, though the size of the impacts is uncertain. In warmer oceans nutrients in deeper water will be less easily recycled to the surface, which may lead to lower biological productivity overall.

On land, wet places, such as much of Southeast Asia, are likely to get wetter, and dry places, such as much of south-ern Africa and the south-western United States, drier. In northern climes some land will become more suitable for farming as springs come sooner, whereas in the tropics and sub tropics some marginal land will become barely inhabitable. These places may be large sources of migra-tion. Such effects are already visible in, for example, the large part of the population of Cote d'Ivoire who come from Burkina Faso.

Increases in average temperature will be less noticeable than those in extremes. According to a comparison of over 20 climate models, by 2050 the probability of a summer warmer than the warmest yet recorded will be between 10% and 50% in much of the world. By 2090 it will be 90% in many places.

## Watching the Weather

People will also have to contend with unpredictable shifts in weather patterns. Many models say the factors that give rise to the Indian monsoon are likely to weaken. The strength of the rainfall within it, though, is likely to rise, because the air will be warmer, and warmer air can hold more water. No one can say how these two trends will play out. Similar uncertainties dog predictions about the great slopping of warmth back and forth across the Pacific known as El Nino and other climatic oscillations. In general, the closer you want to get to firm statements about what is likely to happen, the less adequate current climate science is revealed to be.

It is tempting to imagine that adaptation decisions might wait for models that can provide greater certainty about what might happen where. This is a forlorn hope. Faster computers and new modelling techniques might well pro-vide more details and finer distinctions. But they will not necessarily be more accurate, or capable of being shown to be so: if different models become more precise and as a result their disagreements grow rather than shrink, which are you going to trust? Decisions about adaptation will be made in conditions of pervasive uncertainty. So the trick will be to find ways of adapting to many possible future climates, not to tailor expectations to one future in particular.

Even then, adaptation can help only up to a point. A 2009 review of the cost of warming to the global economy sug-gests that as much as two-thirds of the total cannot be offset through investment in adaptation, and will be felt through higher prices, lower growth and misery regard-less. But adaptation can still achieve a lot.

The best starting point for adaptation is to be rich. It is not foolproof: not even the rich can buy off all hazards, and rich countries and individuals will make poor decisions. The need to restrict farming with subsidised water in a drier southwestern United States does not mean that the political means of doing so will be found before damage is done. But wealth buys information (a lot of people are studying what to do in the southwest) and it opens up options. Resources help people adapt both before the fact, by reducing risks, and after it, by aiding recovery from harm.

Wealth can create hedges against the effects of climate change, even if they are not conceived of as such. Insurance markets are a case in point, though they have flaws: a lack of relevant history makes evolving risks hard to price, and government policies often dampen the signals that would otherwise make people more realistically wary of coasts and floodplains. Public-health systems are another: in better-off countries these did far more to reduce the effects of malaria in the 20th century than warming did to worsen them. Economic development should see improvements in health care that will, in aggregate, swamp the specific infectious-disease threats associated with climate change.

## The Indiscreet Charm of Being Loaded

Rich countries can also afford big, expensive projects. Studies suggest that although much of the Netherlands lies below sea level or is at risk of river flooding, the Dutch can view the prospect of a rising sea level with a certain equanimity, at least for their own land. Plans outlined in 2008 to deal with a rise of more than two metres by 2200, as well as increased winter flow along the Rhine and Meuse rivers, put the cost of holding at bay the worst flood expected for 10,000 years at 1 billion–2 billion ($1.5 billion–3 billion) a year for a century. That is easily affordable.

Other rich coastal areas have considered similar commitments. The Marina Barrage offers Singapore some protection against floods, as well as improving its ability to store fresh water. London has its Thames Barrier, first imagined after floods in 1953. The barrier was intended to deal with the worst flood expected over a millennium or more. That period looks more testing now than when the barrier was built, but Britain's Met Office thinks the barrier, combined with other measures, is pretty much fit for purpose for this century.

New York might, in principle, protect itself against a hurricane-driven storm surge on top of a higher sea level with a much more massive set of barriers that could seal the Verrazano Narrows and the smaller spans of Throgs Neck, at the base of Long Island Sound, and the Arthur Kill, west of Staten Island. However, as Matthew Kahn,

an economist at the University of California, Los Angeles, points out in his book, *Climatopolis*, the politics of such huge and hugely costly engineering might prove difficult. New Amsterdam does not have the attitudes of old Amsterdam.

Poor countries will often lack the financial means, technical expertise or political institutions necessary for such endeavours. Yet they are often at increased risk, principally because they are usually more dependent on farming than rich countries, and no other human activity is so intimately bound up with the weather. Crops are sensitive to changes in patterns of rainfall and peak temperature, as well as to average temperature and precipitation; so are the pests and diseases that attack them.

In its 2007 assessment, the IPCC's picture of agriculture in a warmer world was one of two halves. In low latitudes higher temperatures are likely to shorten growing seasons and stress plants in other ways. In high latitudes, if warming is moderate, growing seasons are expected to lengthen and yields to rise, in part because raised $CO_2$ levels aid photosynthesis.

The IPCC thus sees agriculture as being not too badly affected by 2°C of warming, as long as you stick to global averages. Above that (probably towards the end of the century) things look bad. Some think they look bad well before that. One worry is that a lot of harm may be done if temperatures breach certain thresholds even briefly. A fine-grained analysis of historical data from the United States by Wolfram Schlenker of Columbia University and Michael Roberts of North Carolina State University found such thresholds for maize (corn), soya and cotton, America's largest crops by value. One extremely hot day, their model suggests, can cut annual productivity by 7%. Applying their findings to models of a world with unabated emissions, they found yield declines of 63–82% by the end of the century, with hefty drops even in the relatively clement first half.

This study, like many, made no provision for $CO_2$ fertilisation. The question of how to do so is vexed. If plants grow in chambers with high concentrations of $CO_2$, yields rise a lot (which is why tomato farmers and others use $CO_2$ in their greenhouses). More realistic experiments using carefully contrived sprays of $CO_2$ upwind of crops show a much lower bonus. Remarkably, experiments like this, which provide the nearest analogues to what the world may be like in a few decades' time, are carried out in only a handful of places. None regularly looks at tropical crops.

Against the uncertainty over thresholds and $CO_2$ fertilisation must be weighed farmers' ability to adapt to change and improve yields. Despite many warnings of doom, yields of arable crops have grown remarkably in the past half-century. Among other things, this intensification of farming has saved a great deal of wilderness from the plough: to feed today's population with 1960's yields would require an area of extra farmland roughly as big as Russia. In that it avoids deforestation, intensification is one of a number of adaptation strategies which also help mitigation.

Successful adaptation will require not just expanded research into improved crop yields and tolerance of temperature and water scarcity, but also research into new ways of managing pests, improving and conserving soil, cropping patterns and crop-management techniques that add resilience. Such research—and its application—will make it more likely that enough food for 9 billion people can be grown in a three-degrees-hotter world without much of the planet's remaining uncultivated land or pastures coming under the plough.

If yields cannot be improved sufficiently, though, desperation may lead to more wilderness being uprooted or burned. A headlong rush for biofuels might have similar effects. This would be one of those adaptations to climate change that looked a lot like an adverse impact. Faster loss of species is highly likely in many ecosystems as a result of warming; greatly expanding farmlands will make this worse. It will also add to the fundamental problem, as clearing forests releases greenhouse gases.

## Keeping the Poor Always with Us

Even if the world contrives to keep feeding itself without too much ecosystem damage, many of those dependent on agriculture or in poverty could still suffer a great deal. Regional droughts could wreak havoc, with bad ones causing global surges in food prices.

Many of the millions of poor farming households in poor countries, who make up the bulk of the world's agricultural labour force if not its agricultural output, already face more variable weather than farmers in temperate countries do. That and a lack of social safety-nets makes most of them highly risk-averse, which further limits their ability to undertake some adaptation strategies, such as changing crop varieties and planting patterns. They will often prefer surer chances but lower yields. Worse, in bad weather a whole region's crops suffer together.

Here as elsewhere, there is a role for insurance to transfer and spread the risks. Marshall Burke of the University of California, Berkeley, a specialist in climate impacts, argues that the best agricultural-insurance options for developing countries will pay out not when crops fail (which reduces incentives for the farmer) but when specific climatic events occur, such as rainfall of less than a set level. But getting farmers to invest in such schemes, even with small premiums, is hard. It also requires finding reinsurance for the local insurer, because there is a high chance of a lot of claims coming in at once. What's more, actuarial accounts of future climate risk are necessarily speculative and error-prone.

Farmers may be cheered by the thought that food prices are likely to rise. For poor farmers, who spend much of their income on food, this is a mixed blessing, especially if higher frequencies of drought make prices more volatile too. For poor people more generally, it is even worse news.

Even if prices are higher, crops more resilient and insurance more readily available, abandoning the farm may be the way many farmers choose to adapt. It may be prudent even before the fact. Paul Collier, Gordon Conway and Tony Venables, three British development specialists, have suggested that attempts to provide anticipatory help to poor African farmers could be badly overdone. Better to encourage them into cities and to reform labour markets, restrictions on the opening and closing of firms and so forth in ways that will help them earn money.

More than half the world's people live in cities already. Three-quarters or more may do so by mid-century. Encouraging this trend further, at least in some places, may be a useful way of reducing the economy's exposure to climate change. Statistical analyses by Salvador Barrios of the European Union's Joint Research Centre and his colleagues suggest that climate change is already a factor in African urbanisation. A related study shows strong climate effects on sub-Saharan agriculture in Africa not seen elsewhere, which is not perhaps surprising given the huge effect of the 1980s droughts across the Sahel.

A downside to urbanisation is that cities are hotter than the surrounding countryside, creating what meteorologists call "urban heat islands." But there are ways of dealing with this. More greenery in a city, spread through streets and over roofs, means more cooling as water evaporates from leaves; the bits which are not green can be painted white, to reflect sunlight.

And cities have intrinsic advantages. City dwellers' emissions per person tend to be lower, and the more planners can do to increase population density the better. Protecting a single port city from floods is easier than protecting a similar population spread out along a coastline of fishing villages (though when things go wrong disasters can be correspondingly larger and harder to address). Cities have higher rates of innovation and of developing new businesses, business models and social strategies, formal or informal.

Ideally, there would be opportunities to move to cities in other countries, too; the larger the region in which people can travel, the easier it is to absorb migrants from struggling areas. This is one reason why adaptation is easier for large countries or integrated regions. Within the EU, Greeks and Italians will be better placed to move to cooler climes than inhabitants of similarly sized countries elsewhere.

## Powers of Example

The cost of all this adaptation is hard to judge—and is another area where adaptation and impact become confused. Melissa Dell of the Massachusetts Institute of Technology and her colleagues argue that in developing countries GDP growth has been lower in hotter years than in cooler ones. This may carry over into longer-term increases in temperature. The mechanism is obscure: it may simply be that overheated people work less hard. That can be seen either as adaptation or as a worrying impact, slowing down the economic growth which is the surest foundation for other, more positive adaptations.

If climate change does slow poor countries' growth rates, the onus on rich ones to help will be even larger. This was recognised to some extent in the Copenhagen accord, which proposed that $100 billion a year should flow from north to south by 2020, to be split between investments in mitigation and adaptation. But whereas investments in mitigation are fairly easy to understand—build windmills

not coal-fired power stations, and so on—those in adaptation are harder to grasp. Action on climate bleeds into more general development measures.

The poorest countries all have wish-lists for adaptation funding, drawn up in the UN climate-convention process of which the Copenhagen and Cancun meetings are part. Money and know-how are essential, but so is example. Rich countries can show, through their own programmes for flood defence, zoning laws, sewerage and so on that adaptation must be part of the mainstream of political and economic life, not an eccentric and marginal idea. Adaptation by and for the poor alone is likely to be poor adaptation.

"Facing the Consequences," THE ECONOMIST, November 27–December 3, 2010, pp. 85-88. Reprinted with permission from *The Economist*, obtained via RightsLink.

# 19 TOWARD A NEW AMERICAN ENVIRONMENTALISM

Benjamin Benson

*This is an essay derived from a series of lectures that were delivered to California environmental groups in 2004. The author links America's environmental future to its environmental prehistory. In addition, the author proposes a restructuring of the philosophical foundation of American culture and, by implication, that of other modern industrial cultures. The author has spent years working with Native peoples of California.*

The encompassing environmental challenge that America now faces is that of trying to balance human activities with a sustainable habitat. At present we are failing not only to keep a healthy American landscape but we, and other Western industrial cultures, are now impacting the global ecology. This challenge, although now larger in scale, is not at all new to our land. Other cultures that once managed America also struggled with similar issues, albeit on a smaller regional basis. Fortunately for us it is possible to deconstruct some of America's environmental prehistory and gain insight into our own potential solutions.

Anthropology and archaeology have demonstrated that some Native American cultures failed to sustain their way of life while others could probably have survived indefinitely. Clearly the greatest environmental challenges are faced by cultures with agricultural economies. Farming forces greater production from the habitat and requires greater labor input from people. Farming is always linked to population increase and increasing fragility in the human relationship to the land. A noteworthy prehistoric failure of an agriculturally based civilization is evident in the American Southwest. In the four corners region of Arizona, New Mexico, southern Colorado, and southern Utah, hundreds of Anasazi communities were abandoned about 1300 A.D. Some of the more famous of these are Chaco Canyon and Mesa Verde. Tourists from throughout the world come to marvel at the extraordinary architecture, sophisticated solar and lunar astronomy, and exquisite ceramic art that flourished in the Southwest. But Anasazi culture failed to sustain itself and it collapsed before the arrival of the Spanish. It is important to note that this collapse was not the result of foreign invasion, disease, or any single catastrophic event. Rather it was a systemic, internal collapse, a cultural inability to sustain a viable habitat that would support a large population.

A similar collapse is seen in the Mississippi valley where once there were great pyramids, walled towns, and large, calendrically designed earthworks that were part of a once successful farming culture. Like the Anasazi the prehistoric Mississippians had trade networks that spanned the continent with links to Mexico. But for all their greatness both of these prehistoric American civilizations failed to adequately address that same environmental challenge that we face today. In their demise, both civilizations failed to stem a destructive cultural momentum and they both abandoned their lavish homes. In the case of the Anasazi, the fall was brutal. People were killing and eating each other in the final days at Chaco Canyon.

This same downward trajectory toward cultural failure is also seen in Mesoamerican prehistoric civilizations. Archaeologists continue to investigate the collapse at Teotihuacan in the highlands of Mexico where a huge cultural development descended into violent self-destruction. Similarly the ancient Maya of the Mexican Yucatan, Belize, and Guatemala abandoned many dozens of ceremonial and population centers after periods of internal violence and environmental stress.

In spite of some regional catastrophes, other Native American cultures succeeded in balancing human needs with environmental sustainability. After the fall of the Anasazi, according to several of the author's friends at Hopi, Arizona, the *Hopitu* elders created a sustainable agricultural community in one of the most fragile environments in the America with no creeks, no rivers, or forests. Hopi is America's oldest religiously based collective of people who were assembled from a variety of linguistic groups. Five thousand *Hopitu* or *People of Peace* have managed to live in balance with their habitat with constant population levels for at least seven hundred years. The Hopi environmental management system is fascinating and it provides an important model for us.

Other sustainable cultures had nearly identical principles of achieving homeostasis with the habitat. Good cultural examples are the northern California Pomo and Miwok

who could probably have survived indefinitely had the Euro-Americans not replaced Indian life-ways with a culture that had so little sense for the sacred in Nature at that time. Fortunately enough is known about successful Native American cultural ecology from these groups from which we may still gain knowledge. As we examine these systems of American Indian environmental management we must dismiss the popular but false idea that Indians lived in completely natural, unaltered habitats. That idea is not only false but it creates impossible goals that no culture has ever reached. All human cultures, even small-scale bands and triblets, always modify their habitat to suit their cultural needs. Pomo and Coast Miwok environmental success did not occur by keeping nature unaltered. These cultures modified their habitats in major ways while managing a sustainable environment in which they lived in homeostasis. The most dramatic example is the Pomo and Miwok annual burning of vast sectors of their ecosystem. In so doing they increased the meadowlands while decreasing the brushy chaparral vegetation as well as eliminating many juvenile trees. The burning also enhanced the forage for the deer and increased their populations. The burning made the northern California oak woodland into something akin to a giant park; clearly it was not an untouched wilderness.

In addition, Hopi, Pomo, and Miwok cultures imposed rigid limits on exploitation of the habitat. Planting for the Hopi and hunting and gathering for all three cultures was strictly regulated by elaborate systems of religious controls that limited how much of any resource could be exploited. These rules are still in place at Hopi. Violation of these traditional rules was seen as a moral infraction. At the same time, all three groups controlled their own population levels. Through customs of birth spacing, the use of botanical contraceptives, and religious restrictions on sexuality, they limited their own numbers. But it is very important to emphasize that these cultural limitations on habitat exploitation and population levels were not founded in worldview patterns that resemble Western scientific reasoning. Nor were these native systems consciously understood in an overt way. Rather these limitations were founded in religious and philosophical systems that were taught as a human moral reality. Those cultures that had such limiting measures were those that survived the longest in balance with their habitats.

In Hopi, Pomo, and Miwok cultures, people are taught to recognize a divine essence in every species in nature. Humanity is defined as merely a part of the sacred fabric of interconnected life, not more important than other living beings. Indian children are taught that other life forms must be respected and honored because they too share the divine force of existence. Humans are not the rulers set apart from the environment, but collectively they *are* the environment along with all other precious life. Native customs such as fasting and abstinence at certain times of the year are ways of honoring the sacred essence of nature. Such sacrifices are part of ceremonies that honor nature's gifts with blessings. In the native view, to ignore and dishonor nature will result in eventual destruction of the individual and of society. Sufficient proof of this wisdom is obvious in the failure of the Anasazi, the Mississippians, Teotihuacan, and the classic Maya.

Native American philosophical beliefs that integrate humanity with nature are deeply imbedded cultural values that are expressed in spiritual and religious ritual. The Hopi farmer blesses the earth and sings to the plants in the most heartfelt ceremonial manner. In many native cultures, Indian hunters formally ask the animals to give themselves as sustenance for one's family. The hunter feels obligated to observe cultural restrictions when taking these precious gifts. Likewise the weaver must sing to the basket plants that have been nurtured by generations of weavers in her family. Native American environmental management is not founded in conscious, scientifically based behavior. Instead, ongoing cultural success occurs as a form of natural selection of the most adaptive cultures. Those cultures that last for millennia are those in which people internalize appropriate values and where they practice religiously based limitations on exploitation. Environmentally successful native cultures view nature animistically and engage in a social relationship with other creatures that share their world. Cultures who did not create religiously based systems of limitation often left ruins for later visitors to examine. One Second Mesa kiva priest with the simple words powerfully summarized the Hopi view: "Our way is about *respect*."

When millions of Europeans escaped failing Old World cultures to immigrate to the new "Americas," they ignored some of their life ways that might have given them examples of sustainability. They transplanted many doomed cultural traditions to North America and created their own myth of the limitless possibilities for exploitation of the new land. Perhaps America might now be more ready to assimilate what could have been known before? If native traditions were to be the model, it would require nothing less than a new definition of what it means to be a human being. Consumerism would be replaced with an environmentalism linked to a moral and religious foundation. To follow early native examples, nature must again be granted sacred status. In this context, current behaviors such as clear-cutting a forest habitat or ruining a creek ecosystem would be condemned as unholy.

One of the greatest difficulties for a moral and religious environmentalism to be formed in our time might be the combined resistance from the existing philosophical foundations of consumer culture and its established conservative religious authorities. The religious traditions of the industrial world have often worked to suppress or destroy cultures where nature is seen as an expression of the divine. A departure from current historic dogma and lessening of institutionalized religious power could be perceived as evil by some religious authorities. In one early California example, Junipero Serra saw native nature worship as evil and helped destroy dozens of sustainable cultures.

Ironically, viewing nature as sacred may be the most simple and effective means for the rebirth of sustainability that America now needs and to suggest this is not an attempt to delegitimize established religious thought. Nor is it a recommendation to usurp the traditions of particular native groups, who may regard that as exploitation. This shift in worldview is better seen as a reappraisal and redirection of often suppressed features of major religions. Knowledgeable religious scholars know that by sifting through established texts (Christian, Jewish, Muslim, Hindu, and Buddhist), one can find and embrace a new environmentalism and counter more conservative factions in their traditions. The opportunities for such study and action are many and varied. From a religious perspective, creation is the greatest miracle of all and it is the most immediate and accessible evidence of the divine. Religion, like all aspects of human culture constantly evolves. It is not difficult to begin an emphasis on many great sages as environmental prophets who did the work of the divine by advocating respect for creation. Jesus could be among them and it should be especially easy for Judaism, Hinduism, Buddhism and Taoism to find many similar voices and shift emphasis slightly to recapture their established environmental teachings.

From even this brief examination of native traditions, it appears critical for American environmentalism and for the world, to examine a revitalization of our religious and moral foundations in regard to nature. It seems clear that a new religious environmental emphasis and an alternative set of moral values that mute consumerism could foster and aid a new environmental sustainability.

With a new/ancient definition of what it means to be a human linked to such beliefs, rampant habitat destruction would become "sinful." If a *sacred* American landscape can be saved, perhaps these ethics could be shared in the farther reaches of the earth and a beautiful balance achieved once again.

"Toward a New American Environmentalism" by Benjamin Benson. Reprinted with the permission of the author.

# SECTION V:
*Map Quizzes and Exercises*

# SECTION V: *Map Quizzes and Exercises*

# M A P   Q U I Z

**Name**

**Section**

## Map Quiz #1

Locate the following items on the world map.

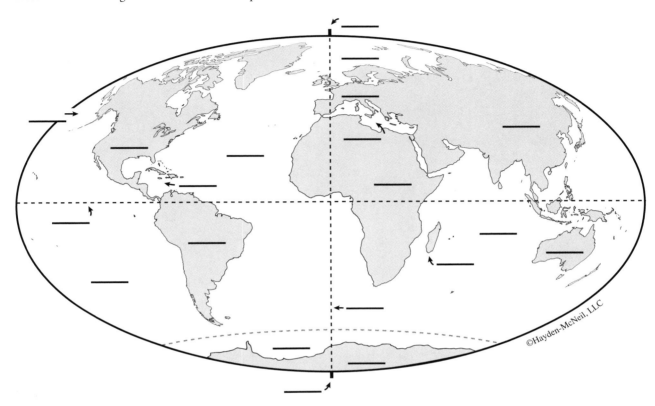

| | |
|---|---|
| 1. Africa | 11. Arctic Ocean |
| 2. North America | 12. Southern Ocean |
| 3. Europe | 13. Indian Ocean |
| 4. Asia | 14. Mediterranean Sea |
| 5. South America | 15. Caribbean Sea |
| 6. Australia | 16. Bering Straits |
| 7. Madagascar | 17. South Pole |
| 8. Antarctica | 18. North Pole |
| 9. Pacific Ocean | 19. Equator |
| 10. Atlantic Ocean | 20. Prime Meridian |

## Map Quiz #2

Locate the following countries, features, or regions on the map found on the following pages. You may be asked to turn this in as an exercise or locate these from memory as a class quiz.

1. The "New World"
2. The "Old World"
3. United States
4. Central America
5. Tierra del Fuego
6. Galapagos Islands
7. Amazon Basin
8. South Africa
9. Rwanda
10. Tanzania
11. Ethiopia
12. Kenya
13. Democratic Republic of the Congo
14. Sahara Desert
15. Siberia
16. India
17. China
18. Java
19. Italy
20. Spain
21. France
22. Germany
23. Portugal
24. England
25. Russia
26. Israel
27. Egypt
28. African Rift Zone
29. Iraq
30. Flores Island

# SECTION V: *Map Quizzes and Exercises*

**Map Quiz #2: World Map—North America and South America**

*You may find it useful to make extra copies of this blank map for use in future study activities.*

©Hayden-McNeil, LLC

**Map Quiz #2: World Map—Europe, Asia, Africa, and Australia**

©Hayden-McNeil, LLC

*You may find it useful to make extra copies of this blank map for use in future study activities.*

# SECTION IV: *Map Quizzes and Exercises*

**Map Quiz #3**

Locate the following fossil sites on the one of the two maps that follow. As determined by your instructor, add one example (genus and species) of a fossil hominid living at each site to the list below. You may be asked to turn this in as homework or locate these from memory as a class quiz.

1.  Taung mine or cave
2.  Swartkrans
3.  Olduvai Gorge
4.  Hadar
5.  Laetoli Footprints
6.  Lake Turkana
7.  Trinil

8.  Zhoukoudian Cave
9.  Flores Island
10. Shanidar Cave
11. Neander Valley
12. Gran Dolina
13. Sima de los Huesos
14. Altamira

15. Amud, Skhul, and Tabun
16. Le Moustier
17. La Chapelle aux Saints
18. Cro-Magnon
19. Klasies River Mouth Caves
20. Lake Mungo

## Map Quiz #3: World Map—Europe, Asia, Africa, and Australia

©Hayden-McNeil, LLC

*You may find it useful to make extra copies of this blank map for use in future study activities.*

## Exercise #2: Building Fundamental Vocabulary

Look up the following and prepare a written definition for your class notes. Use these in a sentence that is appropriate for the subject matter of this class. Your instructor may assign this as an exercise or as preparation for an in-class quiz.

**You or your instructor may
wish to add other useful terms below:**

**Prefixes and suffixes:**

1. anthro-  _____

2. bio-  _____

3. geo-  _____

4. paleo-  _____

5. prima-  _____

6. osteo-  _____

7. -ology  _____

8. homo-  _____

9. hetero-  _____

**Other useful fields or terms:**

10. Palynology  _____

11. Forensic anthropology  _____

12. Ecological  _____

13. Environmental  _____

14. Habitat  _____

17. Mammal  _____

18. Primate  _____

17. Hominid  _____

18. Human  _____

19. Race  _____

20. Culture  _____

21. Adaptive radiation  _____

22. Gradualism  _____

23. Punctuated equilibrium  _____

24. Natural selection  _____

25. Mutation  _____

### Exercise #3: Exploring Race on the Internet

The American Anthropological Association, in collaboration with the Science Museum of Minnesota, has produced an interactive website that illustrates and informs us about how "race" or the concept of race is seen today.

Visit and explore this site:

http://www.understandingrace.org

Click on the icon labeled "Human Variation" located near the center of your screen. Next click on the icon titled "Human Variation Quiz." Take the quiz and see how you do. Once you are done answer the following questions below. Your instructor may ask you to turn these in as homework or part of an exam.

1.   How many questions did you get right?

2.   Which questions and answers most surprised you? Why?

3.   What, if anything, is the most valuable piece of information that you took away from this quiz?

Enjoy or probe the rest of the website as you like. You may find it contains information that will be useful in many college classes, not just anthropology.

# SECTION V: *Map Quizzes and Exercises*

## Exercise #6: The Skull

At the direction of your instructor, label these significant skull parts as an exercise or use this page to prepare for an in-class quiz.

| | | |
|---|---|---|
| 1. Foramen magnum | 6. Maxilla | 11. Molars |
| 2. Frontal | 7. Nasal bone | 12. Incisors |
| 3. Mandible | 8. Occipital | 13. Pre-molars |
| 4. Temporal | 9. Parietal | 14. Zygomatic arch |
| 5. Mastoid process | 10. Canine | 15. Eye orbit |

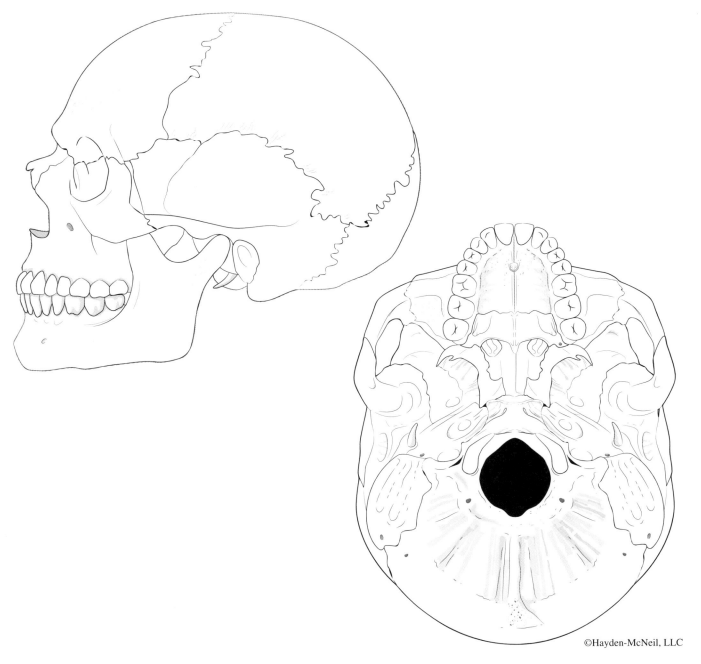

## Exercise #9: Fossil Populations: Early Hominids

| Genus | Species names? | Famous fossils or sites? | Average cranial capacity or range? | Range of dates? | Regions where fossils are found? | Nature of habitat or climate? | Other? |
|---|---|---|---|---|---|---|---|
| Ardipithecus | | | | | | | |
| | | | | | | | |
| | | | | | | | |
| | | | | | | | |
| Australopithecus | | | | | | | |
| | | | | | | | |
| | | | | | | | |
| | | | | | | | |

You may be asked to turn this in as an exercise or provide this data from memory as a classroom exam.

# SECTION V: *Map Quizzes and Exercises*

## Exercise #10: Fossil Populations: Early *Homo*

| Genus and species | Famous fossils or sites? | Average cranial capacity or range? | Range of dates? | Regions where fossils are found? | Nature of habitat or clime? | Tool technology? | Other? |
|---|---|---|---|---|---|---|---|
| *Homo habilis* | | | | | | | |
| *Homo erectus* | | | | | | | |

You may be asked to turn this in as an exercise or provide this data from memory as a classroom exam.

**Exercise #11: Fossil Populations: Neandertals and Modern *Homo sapiens***

| Genus and species | Famous fossils or sites? | Average cranial capacity or range? | Range of dates? | Regions where fossils are found? | Nature of habitat or climate? | Tool technology? | Other? |
|---|---|---|---|---|---|---|---|
| Archaic *Homo sapiens* (Neandertals) | | | | | | | |
| Modern *Homo sapiens* | | | | | | | |

You may be asked to turn this in as an exercise or provide this data from memory as a classroom exam.

# SECTION V: *Map Quizzes and Exercises*

## Exercise #12: Restaurant Visit

You are required to visit *one* of three fastfood restaurants (McDonalds, Taco Bell, or Wendy's), and answer the questions below. Bring this questionnaire with you to the restaurant. Please note, you are not required to purchase any food or beverage for this assignment.

1. Which restaurant did you visit and where is it located?

2. What is the date and time of your visit?

3. Upon arriving at the restaurant, do you see nutritional information presented to the public? If so, where is it placed? *(If you answered yes to this question, skip to Question 5.)*

4. If nutritional information is *not* visible, please ask one of the employees to see a copy of the restaurant's dietary information? From where (if at all) did the employee find the information?

5. Using the nutritional information in front of you answer the following:

    a. Hamburger *or* Beef Soft Taco:
       i. How many calories does a hamburger/taco contain? _____
       ii. How many calories from fat does it contain? _____
       iii. How many grams of saturated fat does the hamburger/taco contain? _____
       iv. What percent of your daily value of saturated fat does it represent? _____

    b. Which item on the menu contains the greatest number of calories? (Please list the number of calories.)

6. What surprises you most about the nutritional information you have in front of you?

7. Have you eaten at this fast food restaurant chain regularly? If so how often and what is your favorite thing(s) to eat? Calculate the number of calories for this meal. If you don't eat here, why not?

8. Did anything surprise you about your restaurant visit?

## Exercise #14: Environmental Quizzes and Games on the Internet

The impact of human lifestyles on our collective global environment and resources is different in distinctive regions and cultures. The Internet provides many ways to quiz ourselves or test our personal "footprint" in terms of the resources our personal lifestyle requires. There are also video clips available to us that enhance our understanding of environmental challenges. Your instructor may assign one or more of the following brief research activities as homework or a study activity:

1. Use the Internet to discover two ways to **"test" your ecological footprint**. List or copy the Web addresses and describe their content in one paragraph.

2. Find and view two **You Tube or similar video shorts** on the Internet that either refine or improve your current understanding of environmental issues OR provoke or amuse you regarding environmental matters. List their titles and Web addresses, along with a paragraph stating how/why the content impacted you.

# ACKNOWLEDGEMENTS

## SECTION I—EVOLUTION AND HUMAN VARIATION

**1. SCIENCE**

"Frauds, Myths and Mysteries," from *Epistemology, How You Know What You Know,* by Kenneth Feder, Chapter 2, pp. 17–43. New York: McGraw-Hill Education. Copyright © 2007 by The McGraw-Hill Companies, Inc.

**2. EVOLUTION**

"Evolution as Fact, Theory and Path," by T. Ryan Gregory, *Evolution: Education and Outreach,* 2008, 1:46–52. Reprinted with permission from Springer, obtained via RightsLink.

**3. EVOLUTION AND DISEASE**

"Evolution and the Origins of Disease" by Randolph M. Nesse and George C. Williams from *Scientific American,* November 1998, pp. 86-93. Reproduced with permission. Copyright © 1998 Scientific American, a division of Nature America, Inc. All rights reserved.

**4. RACE**

"Black, White, Other" by Jonathan Marks, *Natural History,* December 1994, pp. 32–35. Reprinted from *Natural History.* Copyright © 1994 Natural History Magazine, Inc.

## SECTION II—PRIMATOLOGY

**5. CLASSIC PRIMATE STUDY: MOTHERING AND LEARNING**

"Flo and Her Family," from *In the Shadow of Man,* by Jane Goodall. Copyright © 1971 by Hugo and Jane van Lawick-Goodall. Reprinted by permission of Houghton Mifflin Harcourt Publishing Company.

# ACKNOWLEDGEMENTS

**6.  CLASSIC PRIMATE STUDY: WORKING IN THE FIELD**

"Karisoke Field Impressions," from *Gorillas in the Mist*, by Dian Fossey. Copyright © 1983 by Dian Fossey. Reprinted by permission of Houghton Mifflin Harcourt Publishing Company.

**7.  OUR CLOSEST RELATIVES**

"Chimps Grieve as Much as Humans Do," by Elizabeth Weise, *USA Today*, April 27, 2010, p. 7D. Reprinted with permission obtained via RightsLink.

**8.  PRIMATES AND HUMANS: OUR PLACE IN NATURE**

"Are We in Anthropodenial?" by Frans de Waal. *Discover Magazine*, July, 1997, pp. 50–53. Copyright © 1997 by the Walt Disney Company. Reprinted with permission from the author.

**SECTION III—HOMINID EVOLUTION**

**9.  HOMINID ROOTS**

"Ardipithecus Ramidus" by Ann Gibbons, *Science* 18 December 2009: Vol. 326 no. 5960 pp. 1598–1599. Reprinted with permission from *Science*, obtained via RightsLink.

**10. HOMINID WELLSPRING**

"Candidate Human Ancestor from South Africa Sparks Praise and Debate" by Michael Balter, *Science* 9 April 2010: Vol. 328 no. 5975 pp. 154–155. Reprinted with permission from *Science*, obtained via RightsLink.

**11. EARLY MIGRATION**

"Go North, Young Hominid, and Brave the Chilly Winter Weather: Stone Tools in England Hint at Early Arrival of Human Relatives" by Bruce Bower, *Science News* July 31 2010, Vol. 178, #3, pp. 5–6. Reprinted with permission obtained via The Copyright Clearance Center.

**12. THE EVOLUTIONARY ROLE OF COOKING**

"What's Cooking?" *The Economist*, 2/19/09, (from reports by The American Association for the Advancement of Science). Reprinted with permission obtained via RightsLink.

**13. NEANDERTAL KIN**

"Modern People Carry Around Neandertal DNA, Genome Reveals: Team Uncovers Long-Sought Evidence of Interbreeding" by Tina Hesman Saey, *Science News*, June 5, 2010, Vol. 177, #12, pp. 5–6. Reprinted with permission obtained via The Copyright Clearance Center.

**SECTION IV—THE IMPACT OF CULTURE ON HUMAN HEALTH AND THE NATURAL ENVIRONMENT**

**14. LEARNED BEHAVIOR**

"Human Culture as an Evolutionary Force" by Nicholas Wade, *New York Times*. March 2, 2010. Reprinted with permission obtained via RightsLink.

**15. PREHISTORIC POLLUTERS**

"Did Early Man Turn the Outback into a Barren Desert?" by Kate Ravilous, *The Independent*. Copyright © February 25, 2005, by Independent Digital (UK) Ltd. Reprinted with permission.

### 16. FARMING AND THE ENVIRONMENT
"How Prehistoric Farmers Saved Us from New Ice Age" by Robin McKie. Copyright © March 6, 2005, by *The Observer*, London, United Kingdom.

### 17. CHALLENGE IN CHILDBIRTH
"Growing Obesity Increases Perils of Childbirth" Anemona Hartocollis, *New York Times*, June 5, 2010. Reprinted with permission obtained via RightsLink.

### 18. CHALLENGES AHEAD
"Facing the Consequences," *The Economist*, November 27–December 3, 2010, pp. 85–88. Reprinted with permission from The Economist, obtained via RightsLink.

### 19. CULTURE AND SURVIVAL: TRANSFORMATION AND POTENTIAL
"Toward a New American Environmentalism," by Benjamin Benson. Reprinted with the permission of the author.

# ACKNOWLEDGEMENTS